An Inquiring Life

Weekly Contemplations

An Inquiring Life

Weekly Contemplations

Laura Duggan

Nicasio Press • Freestone, California

Copyright © 2008 by Laura Duggan

All sources and quotations are copyright to the publishers listed in the Reference Section

All Rights Reserved

Nicasio Press
Freestone, California
www.NicasioPress.com

To subscribe to future email contemplations, visit
www.InquiringLife.com

This book was typeset in Trajan Pro and ITC Garamond.
Cover photograph © 2008 Constance King
Designed by Constance King Design

ISBN: 978-0-9818636-0-3

In gratitude to my teachers
for their grace and inspiration

"There are four gatekeepers at the entrance to the realm of freedom. They are self-control, spirit of inquiry, contentment, and good company. The wise seeker should diligently cultivate the friendship of these."

The Yoga Vasishta

Table of Contents

Introduction   1
Basics of Meditation   5

Contemplations

1: The Practice of Appreciation   16
2: The Power of Sound   18
3: Contributing to Others   20
4: No Preferences   22
5: Love and Fear   24
6: A Day of Rest   26
7: Handling Obstacles   28
8: Human and Divine   30
9: Enduring Difficulties   32
10: Gentleness   34
11: Choosing the Beneficial   36
12: Motivation   38
13: Dropping Comparisons   40
14: The Influence of Ego   42
15: Accepting Others   44
16: An Inner Life   46
17: Working with Energy   48
18: Change   50
19: Realigning   52
20: Daily Life   54
21: Reconnecting   56
22: Taking Responsibility   58
23: Tranquility   60
24: Choosing Love   62

25: Forgiveness	64
26: The Inner Realms	66
27: Noble Friendship	68
28: Effort and Effortlessness	70
29: Perfect Alignment	72
30: Kindle the Light	74
31: Habit and Discipline	76
32: Flexibility	78
33: Dropping Arguments	80
34: No Complaint	82
35: Dewdrop Life	84
36: Unconditional Love	86
37: Open to Paradox	88
38: Longing	90
39: What is Real?	92
40: Loving-Kindness	94
41: Being Present	96
42: Life's Adventure	98
43: Know the Dark	100
44: Seeing What Is	102
45: Let It Be	104
46: Befriend Yourself	106
47: Liberating Thoughts	108
48: Contentment	110
49: Divine Conversation	112
50: Thinking Well	114
51: Three Questions	116
52: Divine Relationship	118
Closing Blessing	121
Bibliography & References	123
Index of Quotations	127

An Inquiring Life

Introduction

"An unexamined life is not worth living," Socrates declared to a court of judges in 399 BC. With great conviction, Socrates affirmed his responsibility to spend his days in discussion and examination of goodness and other topics. He added that this activity "is really the very best thing that a man (or woman) can do." Almost two millenniums later, I wholeheartedly agree.

Contemplation and self-inquiry have been part of my own spiritual practice for over thirty years, as a complement to a daily practice of meditation. The terms "contemplation" and "self-inquiry" can be considered as two parts of the same process. I use self-inquiry to ask myself questions: Who is feeling this emotion? Where does this thought lead? What is real? How do I understand this teaching? I use contemplation to sit quietly and let the answers arise from within myself.

When I contemplate the spiritual teachings that I read, they become a real and transformative part of my daily life. When I apply contemplation and inquiry to my meditation practice, I am able to observe the effect of meditation on daily events. As I apply contemplation and self-inquiry to emotions and thoughts, I begin to taste a freedom from mental and emotional bondage.

A few years ago, I began to share my practice of contemplation via email with a small group of friends, which slowly expanded to several hundred people. The response to the email contemplations has been quite encouraging. People often comment on the synchronicity of the contemplation with their own life circumstances. These contemplations are now gathered in this small book and offered to you as a support to your own spiritual practice.

The contemplations are best suited for reading one at a time, with an interval of at least **one week** between contemplations. The contemplations are not arranged in any specific order. Feel free to read them in order or at random. Some of the contemplations that refer to particular seasons or holidays can be beneficial at any time. You may find that the quotations themselves take you in a completely new direction. I encourage you find your own way to use the quotations as a springboard for inquiry.

While my own spiritual training is primarily based on the Indian yogic tradition, this book is intentionally nonsectarian. The quotes used for the basis of contemplation are drawn from a wide variety of traditions and authors as a way of acknowledging that all true spiritual traditions point in a similar direction, though their methods may differ.

Many of the contemplations center around some particular aspect of meditation or associated spiritual practice. If you do not yet have a meditation practice, simple instructions are included at the beginning of the book. However, there is no substitute for learning to meditate under the guidance of a meditation teacher. I encourage you to find one if you do not already have a meditation practice.

May the process of contemplation and self-inquiry lead you to greater and greater inner freedom.

With love,
Laura

Basics of Meditation

"How would you like to feel as if you were in love all the time, no matter what the outer circumstances?" With these words thirty years ago, I was invited to begin a practice of meditation. The promise seemed too good to be true, and yet it spoke to the greatest longing in my heart — to live in the state of wholeness and well-being I associate with being in love.

Looking back over the years, in many ways the promise has been met. It is not that I walk around feeling in love all the time. However, with increasing frequency, a feeling of unconditional love arises spontaneously — at the sight of a flower, the sound of a bird flying by, the call from a friend, or simply sitting quietly and meditating.

Essentially what I have learned is that love is not something that exists outside me, but freely springs from within me when it is not blocked by thoughts or emotions. Meditation is the path that leads to the source of love, a love that does not come and go.

Whether we access it constantly or not, once we know the inner place of love, we are never too far away from it.

What is Meditation?

Meditation is not restricted to any one culture or tradition. Almost every spiritual tradition includes some form of meditative practice. The practice of meditation can be as simple as watching your breath or as vast as experiencing the unlimited essence of life itself.

Meditation ultimately transforms your daily life, and yet, at its core, it is very simple. Psalm 46, Verse 10 states very concisely: "Be still and know that I am."

In the fourth century, the great Indian yogic sage Patanjali described meditation as the unbroken flow of awareness to an object of concentration. We all have this capacity for concentration. We use it every day in driving, in working, or in just having a conversation. In meditation, we turn our power of concentration inward.

Meditation as a State

Meditation also defines a state of mind we attain through the practice. This meditative state is an innate capacity, in the same way that we have the ability to go into a deep sleep or a dream state of mind. A meditative state is one in which we are awake, focused, conscious, and yet not perturbed by what is outside us.

In this natural meditative state, we interact with our

world in a profoundly loving and authentic way, present to what is happening and not burdened by concepts and fears from the past or future. This capacity is developed through our formal practice of meditation.

Relax

In today's world, people meditate for a variety of reasons. One of the simplest reasons is simply to learn to relax. Take a minute right now, before reading any further, to just breathe in and out deeply a few times. Take three deep breaths in and out.

Notice what happens as you do this. Inevitably, when you shift to your breath, some form of relaxation takes place. Meditation brings deep relaxation.

The Mind and Meditation

Beyond relaxation, we meditate to work with the mind. The mind can be the greatest obstacle in meditation and our daily life, until we understand it. Through the practice of meditation, we begin to separate from our thoughts and recognize we neither are our mind nor are we controlled by it. Instead, we connect with the power that makes the mind think. We gain choice over the fluctuations of the mind.

Who Are You?

Ultimately, we meditate to know who we really are, the deepest part of us. The Buddhists call this *buddhanature*; the Indian yogic tradition calls it the Self; other traditions call it Spirit. Closer than our own breath, this is the real source of love. This unchanging awareness, or consciousness, has been with us all through the changes of age and circumstance in our life.

We can say, "I am angry. I am scared. I am a lawyer. I am a parent." Regardless of the roles or emotions we are experiencing, the "I am" is the same. This eternal presence is always there, and its blissful and aware nature can be experienced in meditation. When we meditate, our innate nature shines forth.

As we continue to practice, the benefits become part of our daily life: relaxation, a mastery over our thoughts, and a sense of inner freedom. We begin to access our own creativity, and reconnect with our own source of love.

Basics of Meditation

To learn meditation properly, it is essential to attend a class, find a teacher, or at a minimum access some of the excellent books that teach meditation. Meditation is worthy of study in the same way that you might study art or music. Find an expert to guide you. The brief pointers here are a way of encouraging you to begin.

Meditation involves three aspects:
- Posture: how you sit
- Focus: where you place your attention
- Dealing with the mind: how you handle thoughts

Posture

Sitting for meditation entails finding a posture that allows you to be alert and present. The traditional posture is seated on the floor, with crossed legs and a nicely elongated and upright spine. However, it is equally possible to meditate well sitting in a chair.

Wherever you are seated, be sure to have a firm and comfortable seat. Find a way to be at ease and alert. Imagine a string gently drawing your head up slightly.

You can keep your eyes open or closed. If they are open, your gaze is relaxed and somewhat unfocused, not staring or looking, just open and looking lightly ahead. If your eyes are closed, you need to make more of an effort to stay present and not drift off into thoughts or sleep.

It is fine to change positions as you are meditating. Moving is not a sign of failure. Simply maintain awareness as you change your position. If you experience pain in your legs or back, it is better to adjust your posture than spend the entire time meditating on your pain.

Focus

The simplest form of meditation is to place your focus of attention on the breath. There is no need to change your breathing. Just watch it come in and go out.

One way to keep your attention on your breath is to feel the sensation of breath in your body. Where do you feel it? Nostril, chest, and abdomen are a few of the places where it is easiest to sense the breath coming in and going out. Place your attention wherever you can feel the breath. The place may vary from time to time, or even breath to breath.

Focusing on the breath keeps you present in this moment. While you are present with the breath, you are not lost in thoughts.

What does it mean to be present with the breath? A simple analogy is to think of how you do a chore such as unloading the dishwasher. You can have your mind on what you are going to do once the chore is done — cook dinner, put more dishes in the dishwasher, or go out to a movie. Or you can have your mind totally focused on taking the dishes out and putting them where they go.

The same choice is possible with your breath. You can breathe, while thinking about everything else. Or you can be present with each breath. Each moment becomes now, now, now... there is the breath now, and the breath now. A feeling of timelessness may actually arise when you do this.

Dealing with the Mind

The most important insight you can gain from meditation is this: You are not your mind. You are not your thoughts. You are the one who has a mind, has thoughts.

Think of it this way: You say, "My shirt, my hat, my car..." but you never think you and your shirt are the same. If your shirt is dirty, you don't think you are dirty; if your car is bashed, you don't think you are bashed. In the same way, we can say "My mind, my thoughts." If your mind is running wild or your thoughts are up and down, you are not wild or up and down.

In meditation, we learn to break our identification with the mind and thoughts; then, no matter if the mind is happy or sad, bored or not bored, quiet or restless, we can maintain our innate steadiness and freedom. In meditation, we are not concerned with our thoughts; we practice letting them rise and subside without distracting us.

When we are distracted by our thoughts, if we just name them, just let them be, they will disappear. At the moment of the Buddha's enlightenment, Mara, the great demon, kept appearing in various disguises to pull the Buddha out of his state. With each appearance, the Buddha touched the ground and said, "I know you, Mara." And the form of Mara disappeared.

We can do the same with our thoughts. Name each thought that pulls us out of a relaxed, meditative awareness: "I know you, lack of self-worth. I know you, self-righteousness. I know you, boredom." Naming the thoughts, rather than battling with thoughts, allows the thoughts to subside.

The challenge is that we find our thoughts so interesting we don't ever think something more enticing might lie underneath them. All we yearn for — peace, stillness, love — is right there, once we get beyond the thoughts.

The key is not to get involved with a thought, not to judge it or push it away, but simply acknowledge you were thinking, and then move on. One Tibetan master describes it this way: "Do not prolong previous thought. Do not beckon the next or future thought. Rest nakedly in the nature of fresh awareness of the present moment."

If you can do this for even a few moments, you will be amazed at the sense of inner strength that arises from this simple practice.

Beginning Your Practice

It is helpful to set aside the same time each day to meditate. If possible, select a clean and inviting place you can use for meditation every day. Having the same time and place helps you create a habit of meditation.

Begin by meditating for about fifteen minutes each day. You can use a timer, and increase the time as you get familiar with meditating. Keep a journal of your meditation; after each session, note down what happened during the meditation.

Like other practices, such as music or art, you need to keep your inspiration fresh to maintain a lifelong practice of meditation. Inspiration can come in many forms. Reading spiritual books, remembering your intention, meeting with other meditators — all help to refresh your spirit. From time to time, draw inspiration from those who have walked the path and know where it leads. As an old Zen saying goes, if you want to know the way up the mountain, ask the one who walks it every day.

I like to think of meditation as an act of kindness we do for ourselves each day. It is a way of creating an inner shelter from the storms of life and the storms of our own mind. Give yourself this gift.

May your meditations be filled with ease and light.

Weekly Contemplations

1

Every day is a good day.

Zen Master Um-mon Zenji

On the wall by the bottom of the stairs in my house, there is a calligraphy that says, "Good Day." It is an extract from a koan by the tenth century Chinese Zen master Um-mon, who stated, "Every day is a good day." However, the koan leaves unanswered how one goes about making every day a good day. I recently found one possible answer: the practice of appreciation.

The other morning, I woke up thinking of everything I needed to do to welcome some guests that day, and it felt like a burden. I was feeling resentful, a little bit of the "victim." Then I remembered a lecture I had heard the previous day on the practice of appreciation.

The teacher commented that sometimes we begin our day feeling something is missing in our life, and throughout the day we discover nothing is good enough. The food is bad, our friends are annoying, whatever. However, if we start our day with a very short contemplation of appreciating the things in our life, it sets a tone for the day. It reorients our mind. Our list can be very simple: our breath, our bed, our ability to sleep in a bed in a house. And it can extend to other parts of our life that we appreciate.

So, even before getting out of bed, I mentally (and almost halfheartedly, I admit) reviewed a few things I appreciate in my life. Then, once again, I reviewed my day ahead, and I was shocked: the sense of burden had totally disappeared. I realized I now appreciated that my guests were coming and I looked forward to making them comfortable. I also realized I didn't have to be perfect in welcoming them. By feeling my own contentment, I didn't need to please anyone to gain happiness. I was already happy.

I think the most powerful part of all this was the recognition that the state of my mind and my emotional state were totally up to me. I made such a small effort and reaped a huge shift in how I felt.

I offer this as the contemplation for the next week. As you start your meditation practice, take just two or three minutes after you settle in, to contemplate what you appreciate in your life. Let yourself feel that sense of appreciation. Let it deepen and fill you. Then go on to your regular practice. See if the practice of appreciation can make every day a good day.

2

> *Take a music bath once or twice a
> week for a few seasons, and you will
> find that it is to the soul what the
> water-bath is to the body.*
>
> Oliver Wendell Holmes

Last week, I was drawn to a lecture called Music for Healing, held at the local hospital. The speaker quoted a vast body of research about the effects of pure sound on the physical body. One patient who had been somewhat depressed and fatigued gained energy just from chanting sounds. As I listened, something in me snapped awake. I recalled the level of fatigue I had been experiencing for a few months. Immediately I knew why.

For over twenty years, I had been chanting almost every day. A few months ago, not thinking anything was happening, I stopped chanting. Now I realized that since I stopped chanting, my energy had been getting lower and lower. I also understood why I recently had been drawn to listening to classical music. My soul was searching for sustenance.

Rudolf Steiner, a great German philosopher and educator, said, "When the human being hears music, he has a sense of well-being, because these tones harmonize with what he has experienced in the world of his spiritual home."

❧

For the next week, I invite you to experiment with using sound or music as part of your meditation, on a daily basis. It could be listening to Mozart, chanting sacred syllables, or just singing a note. Do it regularly and notice if you feel any difference in your physical, mental, or emotional states at the end of the week.

May your singing bring you great delight.

3

> *We are visitors on this planet. We are here for ninety or one hundred years at the very most. During that period, we must try to do something good, something useful with our lives. If you contribute to other people's happiness, you will find the true goal, the true meaning of life.*
>
> His Holiness the 14th Dalai Lama

This past week, I had the opportunity to attend a two-day public teaching event led by His Holiness the 14th Dalai Lama. On the last afternoon, we were given a blessing card from the Dalai Lama that contained the above quote. There is so much wisdom in these few lines.

The beginning of his quote brings me right to the awareness of our mortality. I have no idea when and how life will end, for myself or those I love. At the same time, it is not a depressing thought, but an energizing one. It moves me to make the most of each day. However, then the question arises: how do I do that? His quote offers one possibility: help others.

The last line of the quote seems to come out of the Dalai Lama's own experience. His entire life is about service. He conveys immense conviction that the Buddhist teachings he presents can help people end suffering and attain happiness.

However, what about my own life? What about your life? What does it mean to contribute to other people's happiness? How much do I have to "do" or how enlightened do I have to "be," for it to count as a contribution? How do I measure my contribution to other people's happiness? I have no answers. Perhaps it is simply a matter of doing it.

※

I share these questions as the contemplation for this week. How are you contributing to the happiness of those around you, in small and big ways, both to people you know well and those you just interact with casually? And how does that relate to your own understanding of a meaningful life?

4

The Way is easy for those who harbor no preferences.

Seng Ts'an, Third Patriarch of Zen,
Hsin-Hsin Ming

Preferences: our likes and dislikes, our opinions about this and that, our expectations. For some people, even the idea of giving up preferences creates immense discomfort. It hints at a bland and colorless life, without passion, without pleasure, without purpose. But is that really so?

We all have preferences. To think otherwise is unrealistic. But we give them up all the time anyway. Because I prefer not to get into traffic jams, I avoid the local highway. However, driving into town today, I chose the highway for the sake of being on time (another preference). Making that simple conscious choice, somehow I felt free of the burden of my aversion to highways. I had opened myself to more possibilities. It felt great to let go like that. Recently, I took a seven-day trip and consciously decided to be totally open to whatever happened. It was one of the easiest, most light-hearted trips I've taken, all because I put preferences aside, at least for seven days.

For me, this quote points towards letting go of strong attachment and strong aversion. To "harbor" our preferences is to cling to them too tightly. Then life in the world is difficult. The opposite, to let them go, is to find that the world can be perfect as it is.

※

I invite you to investigate how your preferences shape your life. Do they keep you from being open to what is happening? Try an experiment for one day: consciously let go of expectations for what will happen that day. Be totally open to whatever arises, and see what happens.

Meditation is also a perfect time to practice letting go of preferences. Regardless of what you hold as your ideal meditation, see if you are able to accept whatever happens in meditation, and let your preferences dissolve. Perhaps we are more than our preferences, after all!

5

Fear always distorts our perceptions and confuses us as to what is going on. Love is the total absence of fear.

Gerald Jampolsky, *Love is Letting Go of Fear*

The other day, I inadvertently restrained my cat at the same time that a neighbor's cat was walking on our property. My cat's need to be free became urgent, and within a moment, he turned his head towards me and hissed as severely as he would to an enemy or total stranger. This very same cat that snuggled next to me each night and nuzzled against my face, now couldn't feel anything but fear.

Of course, when I realized what was happening, I let him go immediately, but not without beginning an inquiry into how fear completely drives love away. I began thinking of my own experiences of fear interfering with expressing love. I also thought about the world situation and how hard it is to ask enemies to love each other when they are intensely involved in fearful situations, such as war. And finally, I wondered, what is it that distinguishes humans from animals? Perhaps it is the capacity, when we find ourselves immersed in fear, to pause and inquire into alternative means of responding.

In Daniel Ladinsky's renderings of the fourteenth century poet Hafiz, he writes:

> Even angels fear that brand of madness
> that arrays itself against the world
> And throws sharp stones and spears into
> the Innocent and into one's self
>
> O I know the way you can get
> If you have not been out drinking Love

The contemplation this week invites you to notice if there are times when your normal capacity to express love is inhibited because of fear. Can you choose a different reaction? What remembrance can help bring you back to love?

6

> *Without going out of your door, you can know the ways of the world. Without peeping through your window, you can see the Ways of Heaven.*
>
> Lao Tzu, *Tao Te Ching*

The past few days have been busy: returning from an extended trip, getting back to work, seeing people. In the midst of this, one person with whom I was trying to connect was unavailable because she was honoring the Sabbath, something she does every week. Just hearing about it made me remember my own experience of taking a "holy" day of rest from the endless stream of weeks and months of activity.

At first, I felt a pang of longing to be in a spiritual community where everyone joins in a Sabbath day. Then, this morning, as I sat to meditate, I realized I already had my Sabbath. Every morning, meditation is a chance to taste the same sweet experience of rest and renewal, but only if I choose to make it so.

As I meditated this morning, I consciously emptied myself of all worldly problems, all the things I normally ponder and investigate. And I consciously let my heart open to a greater presence. Whether you call it God, spirit, consciousness, or Self, there is a presence that is palpable when the mind is quiet and the heart is open. For me, that connection is the sacred purpose of a Sabbath.

❦

For the next week, see if there are ways to create your own Sabbath. It might be during your meditation time or during a daily walk in nature, or a whole day set aside. See what effect it has on the rest of your hours and days.

7

> *You have to pay salutations to your own obstacles, hindrances, because otherwise there would be no notion of freedom and enlightenment.*
>
> Dzigar Kongtrul Rinpoche, *It's Up to You*

How do you handle so-called obstacles in your meditation? The other day, a friend shared that her teenage son was on a meditation retreat. He reported that when he experienced pain in his legs, he thought, "I won't let pain stop me." When he experienced an itch, he thought, "I can be stronger than this." And when he experienced restlessness, he thought, "I don't want to be a restless person." His mom was quite pleased, and rightly so, finding such a wonderful level of commitment in her teen.

I, too, was pleased a teen was learning to meditate. At the same time, I considered how I handle similar situations and began to contemplate the role of will in perseverance. Does the development of a strong will power reduce the size of our ego and sense of doership? Does it lead to a softening and opening of the heart? Is there a more effective way to approach obstacles?

Another approach to obstacles is to use the process of inquiry, which is sometimes called *vipassana*. When we feel pain, inquiring into the pain — that is, looking at it closely, seeing where it is and what it feels like — actually begins to reduce the pain. We don't grin and bear it, but we grin and "bare" it, until we see it for what it is: energy. Ditto for an itch. Restlessness is the same, except it is energy trying to move in the mind, not just the body. When we examine it, we discover it is simply a passing state of mind. In Buddhist terminology, we see things as empty of permanent existence. In the Indian tradition, we see things as a movement of divine energy. Either way, we are freed from it without having to assert our limited will.

For the next week, I invite you to examine how you deal with obstacles in meditation. More importantly, how does your approach spill over into your daily life? How do you deal with obstacles in your life?

8

It seems only yesterday I used to believe
there was nothing beneath my skin but light.
If you cut me I would shine.
But now when I fall upon the sidewalks of life,
I scrape my knees. I bleed.

    Billy Collins, *Sailing Around the Room Alone*

In his usual lighthearted yet profound way, the former poet-laureate Billy Collins captures one of the great mysteries of life. How do we understand that we are both divine, spiritual beings and also quite human? What is the relationship between the transcendental experiences we may have in spiritual practices and living our day-to-day lives?

In my early years of practicing meditation, the transcendental experiences created a sort of metaphysical carrot that lured me to continue to meditate daily. The remembrance of states filled with bliss and peace were a stark contrast to the reality of everyday life. However, as time has gone by, I became aware that if I only value the experiences that take me beyond this body and mind into the realm of the divine, I am creating a serious duality. I do not love simply being human.

Rather than abandoning my limited human self, now I want to call the experience of divine power down into the small self so it feels supported and loved by the highest power. Rather than separating my spiritual and human natures, I long to fully integrate them. Meditation is a great place to practice this.

※

As a practice for the next week, you might envision and feel the divine energy of the heavens pouring into you through the top of your head, embracing and supporting the very human self that is here on this earth. When I do this practice, it feels very comforting and gives me the strength to walk tall in daily life. Perhaps you can make some journal entries about how this works for you.

9

Just remember: you can endure anything your mind can make endurable, by treating it as in your interest to do so.

Marcus Aurelius, *Meditations*

It's amazing to me how great thinkers everywhere come to the same conclusion: everything depends on our mind. The quote from the Roman Emperor Marcus Aurelius could easily have been from any number of wise beings. The words remind me of Shakespeare: "There is nothing either good or bad, but thinking makes it so."

Great words are nice; putting them into practice is the real trick. Recently, I was faced with a situation I thought would be hard to bear. My first instinct was to try to escape somehow. I was quite convinced what I was facing would be more than I could or wanted to handle. Eventually, I discovered the amount of effort involved in the "escape" was far more draining than just bearing the situation. Only then was I able to realize that the situation was actually going to strengthen my own capacities.

For me, one key to the transformation was to remember we are never given more than we are capable of handling. This is closely tied with feeling I am not alone in the universe. A faith in a benevolent power that supports my life seems to free my mind from the grip of fear.

For the next week, when you are facing a difficulty, see if you can decide to make the best of it. What does it take for you to consider it in your interest to go through whatever is facing you? And what happens when you make that shift? You also might apply this to your meditation practice. When it feels as though you just cannot sit for another minute because of restlessness, how can you change your thinking?

10

Nothing is so strong as gentleness, nothing so gentle as real strength.

St. Francis de Sales

I find it intriguing that something as simple as gentleness can sometimes be difficult to manifest. Especially when it comes to being gentle with people who think or act differently than I expect. An ungentle feeling arises: "they have to change." I find myself tightening into a knot of self-righteous indignation and anger. When my expectations are not met, it seems gentleness goes out the window.

It was a great relief to discover I am not alone in finding the practice of gentleness challenging. The Indian classic, the *Bhagavad Gita*, proposes that gentleness is an "austerity of the mind." In other words, it is a yogic practice to restrain harshness of mind. Even when we have moved beyond the need to be defensive, angry, or controlling, we have to break the habit of mentally bristling when something arises. Breaking habits takes work.

Thomas Merton also commented on gentleness, giving a very useful clue about how to break the habit. He writes, "It is in deep solitude that I find the gentleness with which I can truly love my brothers… Solitude and silence teach me to love my brothers for what they are, not for what they say." For me, Merton's words point to the necessity for meditation. When the feeling of mental agitation arises, the best thing I can do is sit quietly with it and allow the energy to subside. Eventually, insight arises, along with a certain amount of humility, as I remember once again that we are all different, and we are all perfect at the same time.

This week, try working with the practice of gentleness in your thoughts, and notice when it is easy and when it is difficult to think gently. How can your meditation practice support you in cultivating gentleness of mind?

11

Both the beneficial and the pleasurable present themselves to man. The wise, having examined both, prefer the beneficial to the pleasurable.

Katha Upanishad

Some mornings, the comfort of my bed is hard to resist. I lie there thinking about meditating, but am reluctant to actually get up and begin my day. Before I know it, time is running out, and I am forced to cut my normal meditation time in half. At those times, the above quote rings in my head. Although the Indian philosophical texts known as the *Upanishads* date back to 500 BC, their wisdom still seems relevant today. Is my lying in bed just pleasurable? Is it in any way beneficial?

It's a provocative quote. How do I know, when faced with a choice of actions, which is going to be beneficial? Is everything that is pleasurable always bad for me? Do I always have to choose that which seems difficult? What is the deeper understanding?

The words from the *Katha Upanishad* challenge us to look at the need for immediate gratification and to give up short-term pleasure for long-term benefits.

It's not easy. This very same *Upanishad* says, "Like a sharp edge of a razor is that path, difficult to tread and hard to cross."

※

I invite you to grapple with this quote and the questions it raises for you. How do you choose the beneficial? What helps you choose? Can you be gentle with yourself when you don't choose the highest good, recognizing the limitations of your own humanity?

As I worked with this quote, I asked a ten-year-old friend of mine what she thought about it. She said, "Getting my braces has not been a pleasure, but I just think about how great my smile will be when I'm done." May we all have such a fresh, young attitude.

12

*Let yourself be silently drawn
by the stronger pull of what you really love.*

Rumi, "An Empty Garlic," *Open Secret*

The previous contemplation about choosing the beneficial over the pleasurable generated some great dialogue among our virtual community. One person from Spain wrote that rather than dwell on her lack of a morning routine, she found other ways to fit meditation into her schedule. Or, as the thirteenth century Sufi poet Rumi says, she let herself "be drawn by the stronger pull." Without the longing to meditate, it's easy to use something else ("I can't get up early") as an excuse not to meditate. Another friend mentioned that even getting up and sitting in a meditation posture doesn't guarantee you will actually move into a deeper state of meditation. The body may be there, but have the heart and mind moved there as well?

Finally, choosing the beneficial over the pleasurable can easily become harsh discipline. Rumi's quote is the perfect antidote to that. We choose something not just for discipline's sake, but because there is something we love even more. In Thomas Merton's words, "If one 'trains' and disciplines his faculties and his whole being, it is in order to deepen and expand his capacity for experience, for awareness, for understanding, for a higher kind of life, a deeper and more authentic life 'in the Spirit.'"

For this week's contemplation, I invite you to consider your motivation in performing any spiritual practice. What draws you at the heart level? What do you love that allows you to continue to choose beneficial practices? How do you keep that love in the forefront of your mind, so each choice is joyful and rewarding? At any choice point you encounter, "let yourself be silently drawn by the stronger pull of what you really love."

13

*When you are content to be simply
yourself, and don't compare or compete,
everybody will respect you.*

Lao Tzu, *The Tao Te Ching*

The other day, I was chanting with a large group of people. I realized I could no longer sing as high as the women were singing. Wanting to sing in harmony, I worked at trying to find my own voice. I went back and forth, high and low, until I could sing at a level comfortable for my throat. It struck me that this need to harmonize, yet remain true to oneself, is true about everything in life, not just singing.

Certain spiritual practices bring this out more than do others. For example, it is pretty easy to harmonize with yourself when you are meditating alone. But, then, what happens when you are meditating in a group? Do your own needs make you self-conscious? What about when you are working with others? It is the same with our beliefs and behaviors. When we have a difference of opinion, do we assume a right and wrong, or can we accept that we are just on different wavelengths? The Zen tradition says it is easy to be a saint on the mountaintop, but coming down into the marketplace is the challenge. How do we keep our own state when confronted with differences?

I find meditation is a helpful way to have conviction about my own goodness. When I experience a basic "okay" state, I can hear feedback and not cringe. I can hear the notes others sing and not have to sing the same.

❧

I invite you to observe your self in the next week and find out what it takes to be content, just being yourself, whether it harmonizes or not, whether it is the same or different. At the same time, can you allow others also to be who they are? How does your world change?

14

Without ego as our primary reference point, mind is naturally open, unconfused, and able to enjoy everything without judgment.

Dzigar Kongtrul Rinpoche, *It's Up To You*

It is traditional during the two-week lunar celebration of the Chinese and Tibetan New Years to offer prayers to remove obstacles. In keeping with that, this week's contemplation is about removing one great big obstacle: the ego.

Is it really possible to become free of the ego? My suspicion is yes, as long as we first begin to recognize it. This past week, as I paid attention, with only a little effort I could clearly identify when I was using the ego as a reference point. For example, not receiving a reply to an email, my mind created all sorts of imagined reactions on the part of the recipient. However, it is quite possible the email was just not that important to the recipient, and there was, in fact, no reaction at all. Another time, hearing a friend share about some plans, I watched my mind jump into action, wanting to find out how I was included. Again, rather than simply listening to the other person and offering support, without putting myself in the picture, I had an ego-based response. In these and so many other small ways, the ego changes the scene, and can often create pain in the process.

When I read Tibetan teacher Dzigar Kongtrul's quote, I was mesmerized. Imagine how life would be if the ego's response was out of the way. I could just enjoy everything: getting no response to an email, hearing about someone else's plans. It would all be delightful.

For the next week, I invite you to watch the interactions you have. See if you can notice when you are open and unbiased, and when you are responding from the influence of ego and self-importance. In meditation, see if there are moments when the sense of the small self dissolves. What is it like in those moments? May this contemplation lead you to a state free of judgment and filled with delight.

15

> *Sometimes too I could see that love is a great room with lots of doors, where we are invited to knock and come in. Though it contains all the world, the sun, moon and stars, it is so small as to be also in our hearts. It is in the hearts of those who choose to come in.*
>
> Wendell Berry, *Hannah Coulter*

The other evening my cat came up to my lap, nudging my hand in a way that indicated his desire to be petted. I complied immediately. It was a moment of pure giving and receiving. The cat came and made a request. I responded. The response came directly from my heart, without any thinking.

In the experience of giving to the cat, I had no expectations of what he should be giving me in return. I just enjoyed the simplicity of the cat expressing his cat nature. I realized I sometimes expect something from the people I care about, such as kind words or smiles, in order to be able to open my heart. Yet, in reality, the softening and opening of the heart is completely up to me. In the same way I open to the presence of a small animal, can I also open to the presence of another, without expectations or demands?

❧

I'd like to invite you to contemplate how you open your heart, irrespective of how another person might be expressing himself or herself in a given moment. Over the next week, notice your interactions with people and see if there are times you can drop your expectations of how others "should be" and love them just as they are.

16

The man who has no inner life is the slave of his surroundings, as the barometer is the obedient servant of the air at rest, and the weathercock is the humble servant of the air in motion.

Henri Frédéric Amiel, *The Journal Intime of Henri-Frédéric Amiel*

While speaking to a friend who was grappling with an unrewarding job, I commented on his patience in sticking it out. He responded, "I do have an inner life." How remarkable to be so aware of the value of his inner life to sustain him through a challenge on the outside.

When I finished the conversation, I began to wonder, do I still have an inner life? With all the activity in my outer life — some satisfying, some not — had I lost the inner connection? That same day, the possibility opened up for me to be alone, without any responsibilities or obligations. I headed to my favorite restaurant on the coast. As I reached a magnificent hilltop overlooking the ocean, tears came unexpectedly. It had been so long since that feeling of awe had arisen. I had taken the beauty of that spot for granted. I immediately parked my car and began to walk the country road.

The sun was bright, the air was clear, the wind was strong, and the ocean draped across the horizon in front of me. The grasses in the fields put on a wonderful show as they danced in unison to the command of the wind, sometimes bending almost flat.

Each cluster of grass had a different color, like dancers arranged in different costumes, some with green hats, some with reddish brown. I was delighted with the world.

Is this my inner life: the ability to revel in nature, see it brimming with life and love? If it comes alive when I am most alone, why all this bending like a pretzel to be occupied with places to go, people to see, and things to do?

Perhaps it is the effort to bend so hard that lets me spring straight back into my natural shape, like the grasses bending with the wind but never losing their innate stately nature. In one short walk, I regained contact with myself as a dreamer, drifting on the golden hills above the sea, with a song of praise in my heart, birds for my companions, and an inner love deeper than any physical connection could ever match.

An inner life? Yes, it's always right there, and it's different for each of us. It is only a matter of honoring the unique way it appears.

I invite you to take time over the next week to become aware of your inner life, whether it appears through formal spiritual practices, time in nature, or in the midst of your daily activities. May it continue to bring life to your life.

17

> *The meditation orientation is not about fixing pain or making it better. It's about looking deeply, into the nature of pain — making use of it in certain ways that might allow us to grow.*
>
> Jon Kabat-Zinn, *Full Catastrophe Living*

In an interview, Jon Kabat-Zinn spoke about three dimensions to pain: the physical experience; the emotional experience, or how we feel about the sensation; and the meaning we attribute to our pain. In his medical work with mindfulness meditation and healing, he addresses all three.

My own practice of working with pain involves looking into pain and seeing the energy at work. In the Chinese system of energy work (*qigong*), pain is often described as blocked energy. In meditation, we have the capacity to engage with the energy and unblock it.

One morning, I rose to meditate with a splitting headache. As I sat, I began to visualize the energy that was throbbing in my head. I mentally moved the energy down my body and out my feet. After circulating the energy in this way for a few minutes, I felt very quiet and was aware that I had lost contact with the headache. I knew it wasn't completely gone. I was just no longer giving it attention to the sensations in my head. I was simply in contact with energy moving through my body. The meditation period gave me much needed rest from the body. When I came out of meditation and noticed the headache pain was still there, I took two aspirin.

❧

I invite you to use part of your meditation time to work with any energy that seems stuck for you. It might be physical or it could be painful emotions. Allow your focus to go to the area where you feel the most sensation. It is important to go to the physical sensation, not the thoughts or emotions you have about the pain.

Visualize the energy beginning to flow downwards through your body and lead it slowly out your feet. When the energy has moved outside your body, imagine it becoming a flow of golden energy. Let this new energy reenter you through the crown of your head and flow down to the starting place. Repeat this process as long as you feel like doing so: let the stuck energy flow out and the golden energy flow in. See what happens.

18

*We must always change,
renew, rejuvenate ourselves;
otherwise we harden.*

Goethe

Saturday morning — a rainy spring morning in Northern California. Unlike the winter rains, this rain has a lilting sound as it hits the fields, the flowering bushes, the world already greened and alive. Unlike the winter rains, this rain delights me as I look out into the misty sky, grateful my newly planted flowers and vegetables will drink their fill.

My usual routine of getting a cup of tea and then meditating is interrupted as I look out the kitchen window, watching the moisture fall ever so gently everywhere. I take my tea, get some breakfast, and sit down at the kitchen table, enjoying the stillness. Formal meditation will have to wait.

A bird lands on the porch outside my kitchen, a surprise visitor. He hops around, looking for something: food? material for a nest? shelter from the rain? I'm delighted watching him come so close, oblivious to my presence inside. Is he free to come now that I don't have my little cat around to guard the house? Did he always come and I just never took the time to notice?

Traditionally, spring is about new life. I realize I can create new life every day, just in the way I go about my usual activities. Today is a good example. Normally I have a self-imposed rigid schedule: get the tea, meditate, and then eat breakfast and begin my day. Breaking that routine today brought me into a new relationship with the world in which I live. Drinking tea in the kitchen and eating breakfast before I step into meditation, everything feels fresh and new. Now I can bring that newness, the sweetness of the day, into my meditation practice and renew it, as well.

For the next week, I invite you to experiment with changing just one small part of your daily routine and see whether it refreshes your spirit and renews your daily life.

19

> *"I always live in this state: I am not this body; I am Consciousness. I lose myself in this awareness most of the time. Sometimes I may come out of this awareness, but I know how to get back into it."*
>
> Swami Muktananda,
> *From the Finite to the Infinite*

There is such profound conviction in the above quote. "I know how to get back into it." How often we lose the awareness of who we are; how miraculous it is to return to it. Do you know how to get back to it? What is your process? Is it something you do, or is it grace? Over the past week, I've wrestled with this question.

After a two-week retreat, I returned to my normal daily routine. The fullness of the retreat stayed with me for at least a week. Then, without warning, my mind crashed into a state of contraction and worry. I blamed my state of mind on the people I love the most. Of course that was absurd, but it lasted a few days. Finally one night, I had a profound dream filled with love. When I woke, I couldn't remember the details, but I was almost back in the same experience I had on my two-week retreat. However, it was not yet solidified.

Filled with renewed energy, I rushed out the door to get the car to the service station for an early morning appointment. I stopped, realizing I hadn't sat for meditation for even one minute. Here's what happened next:

"Okay, one minute to meditate," I told myself and sat down.

Whoosh. As the ninth century sage Shankaracharya wrote, "My mind fell like a hailstone into that vast ocean of consciousness." The world disappeared. All I could feel was the energy pulsing all around me. "Oh, it's not caffeine after all," I observed, "since I haven't even had my tea. No, it's my own Self, vibrating with energy."

Five minutes passed, and I continued to sit. "I'm sure I can get the car fixed whenever I arrive, so what is the hurry? How many times do I rush past this delicious chance to bathe in bliss?" I sat with this deep exploration of God's energy pulsing through me.

Everything in me felt realigned once again. My process of breaking free of the bondage of my thoughts felt complete. I got up and headed to the service station, thoroughly refreshed. Being back in a good state depended on both grace and effort: the grace of my own inner consciousness and my longing to be reunited with my highest Self.

I offer this as a contemplation for you. When you lose the connection with your highest Self, what is your process to realign yourself? How do you maintain your longing for reunion with the divine?

20

*Mornings I hear the sounds of the world;
evenings I hear the sounds of the world.*

Robert Aitken

This week's quote from Robert Aitken captures the sense that we can see our daily life as our practice, moment by moment. His quote is his own paraphrase of a classic Zen line about focusing on the goddess Kuan Yin morning and evening. Aitken makes the point that focusing on Kuan Yin (or God or the divine) puts Kuan Yin outside ourselves. This separates our daily life from our spiritual practice, unintentionally devaluing our daily life.

Recently, when someone asked me what I was doing these days, I had no concrete answer, other than "trying to maintain a good state." While this is true, the answer subtly negates the reality of what I do, such as write contemplations, volunteer for environmental action, provide a sympathetic ear to friends, practice *tai chi* and meditation, and so on. However, I didn't name those because they felt ordinary, because they are not the big things the world values, such as managing this or that, or working at a regular job. I realized I wasn't valuing my own way of living an inquiring life.

How much more positive it feels to eliminate the dualism between my spiritual momentum and my daily life. In a book of essays, one author writes,

"Any event, however small or seemingly trivial, properly attended, opens the door to infinity." It seems to me that a key to an enlightened state is to look at what we do with new eyes, focused on what is present, not on what is missing. Whatever I am doing becomes my path to the divine, if I am willing to see it that way.

As you begin a new week, take time to look at your life as it is. How can you see it with new eyes? How can you see your daily life as your spiritual path? This would be a great topic to write about in a journal.

21

*I know the way you can get
If you have not had a drink from
Love's Hands*

Hafiz, *I Heard God Laughing*

Hafiz, the fourteenth century Sufi mystic and poet, speaks to me across hundreds of years when he describes the state I can get into when I am separated from my own soul, my own source. A contemporary translation by Daniel Ladinsky begins like this:

I know the way you can get
When you have not had a drink of Love:
Your face hardens,
Your sweet muscles cramp.
Children become concerned
About a strange look that appears in your eyes
Which even begins to worry your own mirror and nose.

Humorous, but oh so real, isn't it? Last week, I had a similar experience. One afternoon, I found myself feeling completely empty and sad. It felt like something was wrong. I wandered around the house, wondering what to fix in my life: my work? where I lived? my relationships? By evening, I just gave up and went to sleep discouraged.

During the night, I dreamt I was in a casual conversation with a meditation teacher. When I woke up, all the emptiness was gone. There was nothing to fix anymore. What happened? I realized that being reminded of the spiritual world even casually in my dreams was enough to restore my spirits. Somewhere in the business (busy-ness?) of life, I had lost touch with the inner mystery that feeds my soul.

It is so easy when some uncomfortable feeling arises to try to fix things on the outside. But often the outer discomfort is just a sign of needing "a drink of Love."

The contemplation this week is how to recognize the real source of discontent, and how to reconnect with the inner worlds. What are your own signs of disconnection, and also, what is your remedy? Where do you find that drink of Love?

22

Drive all blames into one.

Atisha, T*he Root Text of Seven Points of Training the Mind*

Recently, I have been contemplating what it means to take responsibility for my emotional world. It began when I noticed anxiety arising in anticipation of an encounter with an old friend. My first instinct was to place the blame on the friend, assuming if the person were different, I would feel better. I created a list of all the ways he needed to learn basic social skills, for example.

It quickly became apparent this was all my own creation. Perhaps I was the one who was lacking in social skills. In fact, I was feeling uptight and nervous rather than open and relaxed. As I examined and understood my feelings, I cleared them up, and also cleared the way for a friendly reunion with my friend.

In the mind training slogans of the tenth century Tibetan teacher Atisha, the instruction is quite direct, with no wiggle room. Drive all blames into one (oneself) means that every time we want to blame anything outside ourselves, we need to turn that around and look at our own contribution.

I find this a really helpful practice. Once I take personal responsibility, I regain power over my own emotional world. However, it is by no means easy. My own experience is that I would rather blame others in order to avoid doing the difficult work of true self-inquiry. One thing that has helped me the most is to recognize that whenever I am blaming someone, I can turn the statement around and see if it applies to me. This is not about blame and guilt but simple honest reflection. With self-reflection, I discover things always change — for the better.

I invite you to practice this for the next week. In any instance in which you put the blame for an emotion on someone outside yourself, see if you can stop and look at your own contribution to the feeling. It may not be comfortable, but it certainly is liberating.

23

Tranquility means the absence of resistance to the experience of the present moment.

Ramesh Balsekar, *Duet of One: The Ashtavakra Gita Dialogue*

The definition of tranquility offered by Balsekar is intriguing. The unspoken implication is that the present moment may or may not be pleasant, yet one can still be tranquil. What do you think?

My own experience is that it sounds easy, but I find it hard to practice. Here's one recent example. I've been struggling with a painful leg injury for a few weeks. This morning, I woke up and found I had no pain. I walked about the house for a few minutes, enjoying the sight of birds on a roof, a cat asleep in my garden, and wild turkeys in the back field. My mind was tranquil and my heart was open. Then, within a few moments, the leg pain returned and the tranquility disappeared, as I experienced frustration, annoyance, and thoughts of "how do I get rid of this?"

More interesting to me than the return of the pain was the experience of watching my mind go from tranquil to untranquil in an instant. I pondered what it would mean to simply accept the present moment, which was discomfort, as equally as I had accepted the earlier moment of freedom. The key seems to be letting go of judging things as acceptable or not acceptable.

❦

I invite you to work with this acceptance of the present experience over the next week. It may be helpful to remember that even the present moment will surely change, as change is the very nature of the universe. What other insights do you have to help you drop resistance and regain tranquility?

May you enjoy a tranquil mind.

24

There is nothing more beautiful and freeing than living with conscious dedication to love.

Gerald May, *The Awakened Heart*

Our previous contemplation on tranquility generated a number of wonderful insights from people. One reader wrote about her "ongoing practice of being happily present in the moment. Recognizing that this moment is all there ever is, I am finding it easier and easier to rest in the tranquility of each moment, regardless of how well it matches my expectations or plans."

For me, the contemplation went one level further than I had been able to go before. Just after I emailed the contemplation, I found myself participating in an event in which my expectations were not met. Tranquility went out the window as my mind became agitated and began complaining. Then I looked up and saw the event organizers engrossed in conversation with great sincerity and good intentions. I realized with a shock that because my needs were not met, I had totally lost sight of my good will and genuine love for the people involved. It was a profound insight about the choices I make to stay in the heart. Later I realized the experience gave me what I needed, even if it was not what I wanted. As much as my ego and pride don't like to admit it, I need to learn more tolerance.

What do we do when our wants, needs, or expectations are not fulfilled? Can we choose love instead?

Choosing love does not mean pretending to like something that I don't like. Rather, it opens me to the paradox of not liking or agreeing with something, and holding onto good will anyway. Gerald May continues the contemplation with these words: "Love is honest, willing to be present to life just as it is, in all its beauty and ugliness. True love is not blind at all; it sees what is and feels it as it is with no rose-colored glasses and no anesthesia."

For the next week, see what your natural response is when your expectations are not met. What does it take to choose love instead? And is there a hidden gift coming to you anyway? May you find yourself choosing love more and more often.

25

*Forgiveness is the key to action
and freedom.*

Hannah Arendt

The subject of forgiveness has been my contemplation for the past few days. At a recent religious gathering, the speaker mentioned that forgiveness had nothing to do with the other person; rather, it was about releasing ourselves from the past. Forgiveness, he said, is not because the other person necessarily deserves it or not, but because we deserve it. We deserve to free ourselves.

I was particularly struck with this idea. Only when I have forgiven something that hurt me in the past, do I have the freedom to move forward. I was also quite taken with the point that whether or not another person knows he or she caused me pain, or apologizes, is totally irrelevant to the act of forgiveness, which takes place solely within my own heart.

On looking deeper into forgiveness, I realize the idea that there is something to forgive contains the seed of blame and judgment: I am right and the other person is wrong. For example, last week, someone arrived at my home for a potluck dinner, with a meat dish, forgetting that I am a vegetarian.

My first thought was that the person should have known better. But the second thought was to understand there was no harm intended, and there was nothing to forgive. As I graciously accepted the dish, and placed it on the table, I felt the freedom to move on. It was a small shift in my own mind that made all the difference.

❧

For the next week, I invite you to join me in examining forgiveness as an energy shift we make within ourselves. Forgiveness can be part of your meditation practice, as you allow the purifying energy of meditation to flow from your heart towards another person or situation you would like to forgive. Then see if you find yourself free to act in new ways.

May your contemplation bring lightness to your life.

26

*The soul should always stand ajar, ready
to welcome the ecstatic experience.*

Emily Dickinson, *The Poems of Emily Dickinson*

Sitting to meditate this morning, my mind was restless and my heart was dry. There were so many other things I wanted to do. Sitting felt as if I were wasting time. I began to rationalize that maybe I expressed my love for God through my actions in the world and didn't really need to meditate. However, rationalization didn't erase the knowledge that under other circumstances, meditation felt sublime. I was feeling restless and disconnected.

As I continued to struggle between meditating and giving up, I remembered a children's story I had just read. A professor teaches three children how to get to a magical land, using their imaginations. They successfully reach the kingdom and are about to meet the magical king, when the professor tells them to go ahead without him. He cannot see the bridge leading to the castle. He realizes his mind is being pulled back by all his worldly responsibilities and he is losing his connection to the magical world. The youngest of the children is able to lead him across the bridge, where they all happily meet the king. Oh, how similar it felt to the meditation experience I was having. I knew the mystical inner world exists, and yet I was unable to reach it.

I patiently made an effort to turn my mind towards

my breath, watching where the breath arises and where it subsides. I imagined the presence of my teacher nearby. I broke the chain of impatience and gently led my mind back to the goal of meditation. Like the innocent child leading the professor, the heart leads the mind.

And like a faithful companion, the sweetness of the mystical lands returned. The sensation of the body dissolved, and the experience of light filled my awareness. Light was everywhere. Breath? Breath became the smallest pulsation of movement in a field of light. Everything in me melted into soft energy floating in consciousness. I felt as if I had drawn a warm bath and finally stepped into it, instead of staring at its surface.

It's easy to think deep meditation is something that happens of its own accord. However, my lesson today is that it takes my own willing effort and patience. The mystical lands are always there; it's up to us to believe in the yearning of our hearts to visit them.

I invite you to contemplate your own practice of meditation for the next week and see how your effort and patience make a difference in keeping your soul "ajar."

27

*He whom one loves will always be near. If
you have entrusted body and soul, there
can be no parting.*

Kabir

Any time I feel alone or without support, the words of the fifteenth century Indian poet Kabir rise up to support me. There is such comfort and conviction in his words. They remind me that the real connection between people is not dependent on physical proximity. When I think of my spiritual teachers, for example, just knowing they have been in my life uplifts me, whether they are near or far, living or passed on.

Tonight I was thinking about the various people in my life who have supported my spiritual journey. I realized that even when I am separated from those whom I care about deeply, I know without a doubt two things: one, they would be at my side in an instant if my life really and literally depended on it; and two, they have utmost confidence in my ability to live my life standing on my own two feet. I was awestruck thinking about the compassion and love expressed when a friend encourages me to live my own life, doesn't create dependency, and doesn't step in to rescue me or cater to temporary emotional states. What a gift we give to others when we express our confidence in them, without conveying a sense of abandoning them.

I offer you these two contemplations for the next week. First, consider the valued people in your life, and see if you can detect the ways in which they encourage you to call on your own inner resources and encourage you to be free and independent, rather than dependent on them. How does that feel?

And second, look for ways you can do this for others. Friendship like this is truly a noble and divine gift.

28

*When effort is needed, effort will appear.
When effortless becomes essential, it will
assert itself. You need not push life about.*

Nisargadatta,
I Am That: Talks with Sri Nisargadatta

The best part of living an inquiring life is that it seems the inspirations that will help me the most always arise at the perfect moment. For example, for the past few weeks, I was filled with a sense of restlessness. I kept filling my mind with the thought "time for a change, time for a change." One morning, I noticed how I followed my usual habit, or addiction, of reading the astrology sites, which also conveyed the same urgency: today is the day, today is the day. My mind was already in gear... what do I need to do to make something happen today?

What would it be like to fill the day with a different energy, I wondered? Someone had mentioned that the Internet had video clips of the twentieth century Indian sage Nisargadatta, so I went online to find them, and got entranced. His words were exactly the balm I needed: "You need not push life about." What a great reminder. I felt a huge burden lift from me, as I relaxed for the first time in days.

As I contemplated my need to make so much effort, I saw that the intensity of my action is in direct proportion to my fear of the unknown. When I don't know what will happen, I want to control it by my efforts. However, it is not the effort that is the problem, but the energetic feeling behind the effort. Action always takes place, but action that arises spontaneously and naturally has a different energetic feeling than action done out of panic or fear.

For the next week, become aware of your own efforts. When are you "pushing life about"? At those times, look more deeply into the motivation. When does effort arise naturally? How does it feel? What is the balance between effort and effortlessness for you? May the contemplation lead you to a sense of true ease in every action.

29

You think to make your living from tailoring
but then somehow money comes in
through goldsmithing
which had never entered your mind
I don't know whether the union I want will come
through my effort, or my giving up effort
or from something completely separate from
anything I do or don't do.

Rumi

The other morning, I woke with a sense of sadness, and the word that arose was alignment. I felt I was out of alignment with my deepest nature, which I sincerely believe is joy, not sadness. Many of us are familiar with the concept of alignment. If our body is in pain and out of alignment, we may seek out a chiropractor or other body worker to realign our body. Meditation is the method I use for realignment of the spirit.

Sometimes in meditation I give the mind the freedom to analyze or inquire. However, as I sat for meditation that morning, I made an extra effort to return my attention to my breath. Stilling the mind became more important for me than following the thread of any thoughts that arose. I was confident that just sitting quietly would allow me to reconnect with my spirit. And, of course, it did.

However, at other times, I need to drop effort all together and learn to relax in meditation. In that state of relaxation, the "union I want" is simply present as a natural state. Effort, no effort, inquiry — they are all valid methods. Then there is simply the grace of meditation itself.

※

As you meditate over the next week, observe the balance between making an effort to still the mind versus using analytical thoughts to gain insights. Which situations in your life call for different approaches? See for yourself what brings about perfect alignment with your soul.

30

> *Kindle the light in your own hearts, and in turn the flame will pass on and light the hearts of others as well. Turn the light of love on those who are in darkness, and touch them with a joyful smile.*
>
> Buddha

The play of darkness and light at the winter holiday time of year is profound. The holiday season celebrates the birth of a great light, even while we live through the darkest days of the year. Yet, no matter how dark it gets, physically or mentally, light always returns. But how does that light return? The Buddha says, "Kindle the light in your own heart." How do we do that?

Another great being, the Sufi poet Hafiz, helps me understand this process of enlightening. He writes, "This is the time for you to deeply compute the impossibility that there is anything but Grace. Now is the season to know that everything you do is sacred."

In other words, when we remember that our very nature is divine, we rekindle the light. When I am agonizing over what I am doing or not doing, filled with self-judgment, I am in the dark. When I wake up to my true nature and act from it, all that I do is sacred. I allow my own light to shine, and I have something to offer others. For me, grace is that moment when I reconnect with the inner light, inner goodness. The winter season is a perfect time to remember that light and spread it.

How do you kindle your own light? How do you share it with others? What happens when you realize that everything you do is already sacred?

May these contemplations support you to bring light and love to yourself and your world.

31

What we consider to be our personality is only a collection of habits that are driving us to our destiny.

Bhante Bodhidhamma, *Buddhadharma Magazine*

Coming across this quote in a contemporary magazine, I began to contemplate habits and their effect on my life. My observation of habits started with my cat. I usually feed him upstairs, but on occasion I put the food downstairs. He goes to the bowl, takes a few bites, then turns away as if it were not to his liking. As soon as I move the same bowl with the same food upstairs to his habitual eating spot, he eats with enthusiasm. It seems to me his habit keeps him from tasting and enjoying his good food.

I began to wonder what habits of my mind keep me from enjoying the nourishment in my life. For example, I used to lead a very structured life. Now I have a lot of unstructured time. Yet sometimes, rather than enjoying the free time I have, I begin to miss the habitual busy-ness to which I was accustomed. The recollection of past habits robs me of the enjoyment of the present moment. Equally useless is when I hold onto habitual thoughts about a person or situation and am unable to recognize that perhaps things have changed.

At the same time, I have a habit of meditating each day. It keeps me focused on what gives my life meaning.

I can't imagine starting my day without meditation. As the Greek philosopher Socrates explains, "The soul, like the body, accepts by practice whatever habit one wishes it to contact." I wonder if there is a difference between the discipline of meditation and the habit of meditation?

I invite you to contemplate your own life through the lens of habit and discipline. What is serving to free you and what creates shackles and limits you? If, as the quote above says, habits drive us to our destiny, what destiny are you driving towards? Take some time to journal your discoveries.

32

To follow the spiritual path authentically is to die to our old rigidities, turning long-cherished opinions and ingrained attitudes upside down... to see beyond delusion to reality... challenging the way we look at everything.

Monks of New Skete, *In the Spirit of Happiness*

Sometimes I think the most spiritual thing we can do is to lighten up. That was the conclusion I came to the other day when I experienced a major collision between reality and my imagination.

I had created a very vivid scene in my mind of my newly born godchild being quietly nurtured by his loving parents, as they rested and sat quietly watching this new miracle in their lives. I even hesitated to call for fear of disturbing this very special and intimate time. I sat to meditate in order to better prepare myself for a quiet phone call. Then I phoned their cell phone, to insure that the ringing of their house phone wouldn't disturb their quiet.

You can imagine, perhaps, what a setup I had already created. The phone was answered and all I could hear was street noise and chaos. "Where are you?" I asked. Parents and newborn baby were at a restaurant, entertaining their out-of-town relatives who had just arrived. It was clearly not a time to talk, and as I hung up, I literally felt a crack go through my system.

It was a most vivid moment experiencing that my reality was totally disconnected from anyone else's reality. It felt like the crack of a Zen master on my back saying, "Wake up!" It was also a profound moment of choice. I could make the parents wrong to cover my own embarrassed state or accept responsibility for my delusion.

I returned to my meditation, named all the thoughts that arose, and simply had to let them all go. I could see the reality: young and energetic parents who were thrilled to bring their new baby to the world. Most importantly, a tiny bit of space opened in me where I could laugh at the whole thing. The ego had been caught red-handed and had to surrender. The spaciousness of letting it all go was huge.

The words of this week's quote capture the process well. What has been challenged is the delusion that I know what is right for others, or even that there is a right and wrong way to do things. Rather, there is simply a choice, moment by moment, to see what is real, and open fully to it.

For the next week, if you come across any instance in which reality doesn't match your expectation, see if you can explore ways to open to something new. Allow things to be other than you want or believe, and let go of the sense of self-righteousness in the process. Enjoy the blessings that come from flexibility.

33

When one gets older, one realizes the futility of a life wasted in argument when it should be given entirely to love.

Thomas Merton, *Follow the Ecstasy, the Hermitage Years of Thomas Merton*

Recently I read a biography of Thomas Merton, which had many wonderful passages to contemplate. Merton wrote on so many topics: contentment, surrendering the ego, commitment to the interior life, and more. Yet, like all contemplatives, he comes back to one principle: love.

I was startled at the way Merton contrasts love with argument. I had never considered that before, growing up in an environment where arguing was as common as breathing. I immediately thought of the argument I was having in my own mind with a dear friend, internally wanting him to change his behavior. This certainly was not loving him just as he was. Upon reading Merton's words, I mentally put down my "weapons" and redirected my thoughts to my friend's good qualities… at least for a moment!

It is easy to argue for our opinions, point of view, preferences, you name it. The argument can be loud and direct or subtle, holding an inner stance that the other person is wrong. Whatever the form, Merton claims argument is in opposition to love.

The Vedic tradition talks about different modes of arguments: *jalpa* is arguing for victory, to prove someone is wrong; *vada* is arguing for truth. Alas, most of the time what we consider to be truth is merely our opinion about something. We lose sight of the truth of Oneness, lost in the duality of right and wrong.

I invite you to work with this quote for the next week. Whenever the temptation to argue arises, inwardly or outwardly, can you catch yourself? What would happen if you dropped the argument? Are you willing to drop into the heart and let things just be?

These additional words from Thomas Merton can support your contemplation: "The deepest level of communication is not communication but communion. It is wordless. It is beyond words. It is beyond speech. It is beyond concepts. Not that we discover a new unity. We discover an older unity. My dear brothers, we are already one. But we imagine that we are not. What we have to recover is our original unity. What we have to be is what we are."

34

Through the practice of meditation, we begin to find that within ourselves there is no fundamental complaint about anything or anyone at all.

Chogyam Trungpa, *Shambhala, The Sacred Path of the Warrior*

Trungpa's statement has a certain outrageousness, doesn't it? The mind says, "What do you mean, no complaint? What about so and so, and the way he acts; what about that other person?" What is more outrageous than Trungpa's claim is the fact that it is true and is something we can experience for ourselves.

Over the past few weeks, I have been discovering this for myself. One morning, I was mentally complaining about circumstances in my life. When I sat for meditation, I connected inside to my heart and its immense peace. In that sweet state, an insight arose, clear and lucid: "This state cannot be diminished by what happens. This state cannot be increased by what happens, either. This state has nothing to do with anything outside me." I came out of meditation startled at the simplicity of this recognition. Connecting with the place of the heart in meditation had totally removed any complaints. My life felt perfect.

Since that time, I have been cultivating the practice of remembering. Each time I find myself carrying negative energy, I make a note of it. At the first opportunity, I meditate for just a few minutes to reconnect with my heart. The experience of "basic goodness," as Trungpa refers to our nature, is still there. It hasn't gone away, and in fact, it can't go away. It is who I am. When reconnecting with that state, the negativities feel like a dream, a superimposition. As I touch my own stillness and witness the complaints or negative thoughts, they lose their power.

For the next week, I invite you to work with the practice of meditation as a way of realigning yourself with the basic goodness in your world. Whether you have a formal practice of meditation or simply practice mindfulness in nature, let yourself touch your basic nature and see what happens to any complaints. Remember to be patient and gentle, no matter what happens.

35

*The world of dew
is the world of dew,
And yet, and yet –*

Issa, *The Essential Haiku*

Last week, I went for a long and solitary walk on a ridge high above the ocean. In the midst of pasture and farmland there was no sound of human activity. At one location, the vista across the ocean to the horizon was so vast and unimpeded that I could actually see the curvature of the earth. I was pulled up to the viewpoint from space, looking down on this planet Earth. I saw myself as a small speck on the planet. My time on this planet felt like a drop in eternity. I laughed as I realized how seriously I take my life, my ups and downs, and yet how insignificant they are in the greater scheme of things.

This was not a depressing turn of events, but rather a liberating and humbling experience. The world's spiritual traditions tell us our life is a dream, or as Issa calls it, "a dewdrop." Yet it is also very real. We often experience this very poignantly when we are with someone at the end of his or her life. Whatever was important shrinks into the background, compared with the transience of life. Then life resumes again with all its sound and fury.

What do we do with this paradox, this dewdrop of our life?

❧

For the next week, I invite you to explore your own relationship with the reality of your life. How do you draw on your wellspring of enthusiasm for life, while simultaneously remembering the fragility of life? Here's a clue from another sage, Kahlil Gibran: "The image of the morning sun in a dewdrop is not less than the sun. The reflection of life in your soul is not less than life."

36

If we make our goal to live a life of compassion and unconditional love, then the world will indeed become a garden where all kinds of flowers can bloom and grow.

Elisabeth Kubler-Ross, *On Life After Death*

The past few weeks have brought me interesting opportunities for deep self-inquiry. It began when I told myself the purpose of my life was to learn unconditional love. I didn't realize the immensity of that commitment. Within days, I began noticing all the many ways I did the opposite. Rather than offering love to people in my life, I watched with dismay the ways I judged, criticized, and unintentionally alienated people. The path to unconditional love became much more complicated than I anticipated.

What makes the practice of unconditional love so challenging? One reason is that my original concept was very small. Unconditional love meant I would love the people I already loved, unconditionally. I wouldn't let petty things affect my love for them. I soon realized the spiritual practice of unconditional love included everyone: people I didn't know very well, people who irritated me, people who disagreed with me, and... myself, too.

What does it mean to have unconditional love? I don't know. I do know the difference between having an open heart and a closed heart. I do know my thoughts create concepts about others that veil reality. I do know my thoughts are my choice. When the thoughts disappear, I can open to others more fully. More than this, I do not know.

So my conclusion is, perhaps I am trying to leap too high all at once. I'm working now on learning unconditional friendliness, which perhaps can lead me closer to the ideal, while taking into account the reality of who I am.

For the next week, I invite you to contemplate what unconditional love means to you. In what ways do you already practice it? In what ways do you already receive it? You may feel this practice is unrealistic, and that you would just like to practice being human. That's also an option.

As you embark on this contemplation, keep in mind these additional words from Kubler-Ross: "The ultimate lesson all of us have to learn is unconditional love, which includes not only others but ourselves as well." Perhaps that is the best place to start.

37

> *The capacity for paradox is the measure of spiritual strength and the surest sign of maturity. To advance from opposition (always a quarrel) to paradox (always holy) is to make a leap of consciousness.*
>
> Robert Johnson, *Owning Your Own Shadow*

The other day, I shared with a friend that cultivating unconditional love seemed to be the purpose of my life. He responded, and rightly so, that there could be a lot of ego present in that kind of goal. Was I offering love to others so the small me, Laura, could be satisfied, could feel good? The alternative, he proposed, was to become empty, to dissolve the small self. Once the ego was dissolved, unconditional love would arise of itself.

While his words sounded convincing, they left me unsettled. My experience was that cultivating unconditional love removed unnecessary suffering for others and myself. At the same time, it was clear this small self was far from being erased. I kept chewing on the question, "How should I practice?" And, I must admit, I was also hung up on the idea of right and wrong, wanting to make one of us right and the other wrong... surely a sign the small self was leading this inquiry.

Much to my delight, both of these dilemmas were answered when I began reading a commentary on the *Heart Sutra*. The sutra starts with the insight that everything is empty (of inherent, permanent, independent existence). Shariputra, disciple of the Buddha, asks, "Then how should we practice?" The answer in the sutra is worthy of deep study: "Form is emptiness; emptiness also is form. Emptiness does not differ from form, form does not differ from emptiness."

The *Heart Sutra* presents the ultimate spiritual paradox. At the same time that we recognize that everything arises out of "emptiness" (or the space of consciousness), we still have to relate to everything that is arising. Even as I dissolve the ego (form) and rest in my own essential nature (emptiness, spaciousness), I can relate to the world and those around me with unconditional love.

What stands out for me in this process is learning to grapple with differences, rather than dismissing them. Through an interaction with a different point of view, my practice was enhanced.

For the next week, I invite you to practice listening to what your own soul says, as well as listening to those around you. Can you find the truth in other points of view, without abandoning what is true to you? How do you handle paradox?

38

Our longing, if we dare to follow it all the way, is what turns us inside out until we find the sun and the moon and stars inside.

Peter and Maria Kingsley, *Parabola Magazine*

The other day, reviewing my current life circumstance, I recognized that, on the outside, it appeared to be quite full and complete. Yet, there was a profound sense of something missing. I experienced it as a discontent, as if my soul was longing for something unknown. As I contemplated all the ways I might change my life, I happened to read the current issue of *Parabola Magazine*. The theme was Absence and Longing. I was flooded with the recognition that the sense of discontent was the very call of my soul for union. Nothing was wrong with my life; nothing needed fixing. It was more about recognizing the longing that is behind all my experiences of incompleteness.

What was neat was that nothing in my life changed. I still had a sense of missing something, but now that feeling became a joy to me, reminding me that the context of my life was the search for the divine, *Buddhanature*, the Self. As the poet Kabir once wrote, "God is in your search."

In many spiritual traditions, longing for union, longing for enlightenment, is considered an essential part of the path. In the Indian philosophy of Vedanta, *mumukshutva*, longing for liberation, is a prerequisite for starting on the spiritual path. Without a longing to reach the goal, we have no incentive to keep walking. To me, longing feels like an inner flame that illuminates the path. Without it, everything appears dark.

For the next week, if you find yourself feeling a lack of any sort, rather than attempt to fix it directly, try to identify the deeper longing that might be underneath the feeling. See if you can stay with the longing, and let it take you where it wants.

39

Come, join the courageous,
Who have no choice
But to bet their entire world
That indeed,
Indeed, God is Real.

Hafiz, "A Golden Compass,"
I Heard God Laughing

What does the Sufi poet Hafiz mean when he says, "Bet their entire world?" And what does he mean, "God is real?" It is amazing how one line of poetry can be open to so many possibilities.

God is a word that can stop many people from even reading any further. However, recently I read a way of describing God as "whatever you believe the highest principle in the universe to be." We all believe in something. We could be materialists, who believe the physical world is the beginning and end of it. In that case, our God is material. Or we could believe in emptiness, as in the Buddhist tradition. And emptiness becomes our God. For Sufis, God is love. I think Hafiz is pointing to the fact that no matter what you believe in, when you believe in it, you will put everything up against it. But how do we know our "God" is real?

One way is when it is put to the test in our life. Two weeks ago, in a sudden and unexpected event, my dear cat lost his life. I was sad, bereaved, and bereft. Simultaneously, I felt surrounded by pure love, the presence of the divine. I knew without a doubt there was a power greater than birth and death, good and bad — a benevolent hand of the universe, rearranging my world. While the event was not something I ever wished for, I had a deep trust it would be for the good of all. In that moment, I was able to bet my entire world that, indeed, God is real, love is real. It was a moment of courage, choosing to move to the highest way of viewing things, despite the sadness of it.

The contemplation this week is to work with Hafiz's words. What is it that you believe in? How do you know it is real? And how does that knowledge affect your life? May the contemplation reveal the benevolence that truly lies at the heart of this world.

40

Love the animals, love the plants, love everything. If you love everything, you will perceive the divine mystery in things. Once you perceive it, you will begin to comprehend it better everyday. And you will come to love the whole world with an all-embracing love.

Fyodor Dostoyevsky, *The Brothers Karamazov*

This weekend, I immersed myself in the practice of *metta,* or loving-kindness. I discovered it takes practice and effort to love everything, beginning with oneself. Although we are born with open, loving, hearts, somewhere along the way we begin to love some things and not others, love some people and not others. Worst of all, sometimes we forget to love ourselves. It actually takes effort to undo this habit and have a genuine open heart.

The *metta* practice is very simple. Many books have been written on the subject, but the basis is to wish yourself and others well by thinking, "May you be happy. May you be healthy. May you be safe. May you be at ease." As I directed these thoughts to myself, to the people around me, even to the fly buzzing around my head, I was replacing old thought patterns with new ones. I felt much lighter and open after immersing myself in these thoughts of loving-kindness all day.

I invite you to explore the practice of sending kind thoughts to yourself and others for the next week, perhaps adding it to the beginning or end of your meditation practice. Even if you don't feel different, the practice of thinking kind thoughts is truly beneficial. May you be happy, safe, healthy, and at ease!

41

> *Instead of trying to see everything*
> *through the prism of the mind*
> *let the brilliant rays*
> *of the eye of the heart*
> *reflect everything in its true colors.*
>
> Gurumayi Chidvilasananda, "Through the Eye
> of the Heart" *Smile, Smile, Smile! Poems*

As I look over my journal notes from the last few weeks, the theme that emerges is about staying present, in touch with my own body, energy, and heart. Once again, I am amazed at how easily I lose these tender connections and how I spend so much time lost in the "prism of the mind."

The other day, I was immersed in wrapping gifts and deciding what to give to whom. I got stuck on the right gift for one of my dearest friends, arguing with myself back and forth. In the midst of this season of joy, I was dredging up old grievances. In frustration, I decided to take a walk on the country road near my house. I hadn't walked there in weeks.

Reaching the top of the incline, I looked back to see the green hills blazing with the last rays of golden sunlight. The cows gathered in a loose group on the farm across the way. In my line of sight were rolling hills, stretching out to the horizon. A verdant green blessed land. "This is my Ireland," I said to myself. "This is my New Zealand. This is my heart's desire, wherever I have sought it. Here it is, at my feet."

I felt as though I were waking up from a dream. I was completely present; all my senses were alive. Where had I been and what had I been doing that kept me too busy to walk this lovely country road? All I could want is available in this present moment, and yet I tend to drift so far away, if not physically, then mentally.

I looked up at the sky to see two blackbirds soaring high above on the same air current. They flew together, yet apart, each leaving its own tracks in the sky. They finally disappeared from my view. I thought of the friend whose gift I was struggling with, and my heart softened. Feelings of love, generosity, and forgiveness arose. I walked back home with a clear mind, deeply at peace with myself.

What does it take to keep love blazing? Is it really that difficult to keep the heart open and soft, to stay in love with the world, with the people in it? Or does the mind just make it appear difficult?

During a busy season, perhaps this can be a constant contemplation: Am I present right now, in touch with my heart, or lost in the mind? Am I aware of my body? Are my senses taking in the world? Can I feel the love that exists in my own heart? May this contemplation fill your week with infinite joy.

42

> *We cannot stay home all our lives — we must present ourselves to the world, and look upon it as an adventure.*
>
> Beatrix Potter, *Miss Potter*

Imagine being brave enough to live the life of your dreams, no matter what your society or culture dictate. Beatrix Potter, living in England in the 1800s, was an artist who stepped out of her world's expectations into the world of her own choosing. She drew with all her heart what she saw with her heart, and the result has delighted children for over a hundred years.

I'm particularly struck by the idea of looking at life as an adventure. To me, it means not knowing what is around the next corner. Or, as the Zen masters would say, living with "only don't know." Living not with fear of the unknown, but delight in it. We don't know what will come of our efforts in any part of our life. However, the adventure of it allows us to take the next step, and the next step and the next.

As I began working on this book of contemplations, I realized I had no idea where it would lead. Would I publish it? What would it lead to in my life's work? Most importantly, was I willing to step out into the world and say, "This is who I am, this is how I live"?

The questions ultimately led me to see the spiritual necessity of standing fast in my own sense of value, without looking to others for affirmation.

❧

I invite you to use the next week to reflect on your own courage to present yourself to the world as you truly are. What does "stepping out into the world" look like in your life? How can you express your own wonder and gratitude for the adventure called your life?

May the world benefit from your own shining presence.

43

To go in the dark with a light
is to know the light.
To know the dark, go dark.
Go without sight...
and know that the dark, too,
blooms and sings,
and is traveled by dark feet
and dark wings.

Wendell Berry, *Collected Poems*

In December, at the same time much of the world gets ready for outer celebrations, it is also a time for inner celebration and reflection. It is fascinating to see how we know this intuitively, if not consciously. One friend told me she began reading through her dream journals, looking at what she has learned. Another friend shared he only felt like resting and meditating, and didn't have much outward energy.

I find the dark days and nights of the winter solstice create a kind of sanctity that supports this need for reflection. Last week, I spontaneously brought out all the journals I've kept for thirteen years and began culling their contents. I love watching the sun set early, having a warm bowl of soup by the fire, and then slowly reading through one of the old journals, seeing what has changed and what is still the same in my life.

At an Advent program I attended, one person described this season as the season of waiting. She also spoke of this season as heralding both birth and death, saying, "There is always something dying, and something being born, in each of us. What we do with that makes all the difference."

As we prepare for the outer celebrations, I invite you to prepare inwardly for whatever is waiting to be born and what might be dying: old habits, outworn mental tendencies. In what way have you felt drawn to respond to the call of nature's inward energy, to enter the dark?

Meditation can be a potent force at this time, as you clear your mind of thoughts and watch what arises. If you can give yourself permission during this solstice season to be still, you may find the inner and outer begin to resonate together. "Know that the dark, too, blooms and sings."

44

Enlightenment is not imagining figures of light but making the darkness conscious.

Carl Jung

On Friday, I woke and started a fire in the wood stove, as usual. I took a warm bath, as usual. I poured myself a cup of my favorite green tea, as usual. I turned on my computer to type some notes, as usual.

However, none of the usual activities relieved my heavy and downcast feelings. The one difference in my daily routine was that I had been without electricity for twenty-four hours due to a winter storm.

As I sat sipping tea, I tried to rationally regain a sense of lightheartedness. In reality, I barely missed the electricity. Surely I could live without checking emails for a day; in fact, I could make it into a retreat, I told myself.

Ah, but the grumbling mind still remained. Was it because I hadn't chosen to be without lights? But I don't choose the millions of events that happen to and around me on a daily basis, such as traffic lights turning red or the sun rising.

Despite all my analyses of the situation, I was still unable to summon up an enlightened state of mind. Later that afternoon, a friend called from across the country. Hearing my state of mind, she advised, "Don't spend another night alone in the house. Stay with friends."

Her words woke me up so I could look at the real source of my mental state: I was feeling vulnerable and alone. As soon as I acknowledged how I felt, my mood lightened up. Minutes later, one friend called to invite me over, and other friends called to say they would come to my house. The evening, which had seemed so dismal, felt like a party!

My insight from this experience was that rather than philosophize or rationalize about outside circumstances, I have to address my feelings directly. It is so easy to blame things on what is going on outside, and forget to look inward. A dark, or unexamined, state of mind is far more threatening than a darkened house. The way out, as Jung said, is by entering the darkness and seeing it for what it is.

The next time something arises on the outside that disturbs your state of mind, is there a way to gain some perspective? Can you see it for what it is and find the inner source of the discomfort, without adding unnecessary drama? As Bodhidharma, the Chinese patriarch of Zen, said, "Not creating delusions is enlightenment." Now there's a great practice.

May your contemplation be filled with light!

45

> *Love does not seek her own way, is not easily provoked, is not anxious to suspect evil... bears all things, believes all things, hopes all things, endures all things.*
>
> St. Paul

Recently, at a workshop called Harmony with Horses, as I approached a horse to interact, he walked away. My immediate reaction was to think he didn't want to play with me. The facilitator said, "How do you know what the horse is thinking? We make so many assumptions. We assume we know what people half way around the world are thinking." I realized I had assumed the worst about the horse, and about myself. It made me think about assumptions I make in my relationships with people.

In each of my close relationships, I can create some story about what a particular action means and act based on my assumption. Recently, when a friend remained silent after I had written a heartfelt letter, I suspected the worst. I assumed I was being judged or criticized. Because my experience with the horse was fresh in my mind, I was able to drop the feelings and simply wait to see what would happen. As it turned out, my friend was taking time to craft a sensitive response. The assumptions I made came from my own lack of confidence. Whenever I realize that, it is easier to let them go. How much better it feels to rest in the state of love, believing in and hoping for the best.

Another friend shared that when she didn't hear from a client for weeks, she assumed the client was displeased with her work. As it turned out, the client had total trust in my friend and had gone on vacation, confident the job would be completed as needed.

For the next week, I invite you to try something different. When something happens that is unexpected or unwanted, try just letting it be. No story. No judgment. No reaction. Just an observation: "Oh, this happened." Allow your heart to soften and assume the best. See what happens to your state of mind when you allow love to prevail.

46

One is not a hero who defeats a mighty army. The true hero is the one who crosses the ocean known as the mind and the senses... You are your own friend; you are your own enemy.

The Yoga Vasishta

It takes courage to acknowledge our own basic goodness. And it takes effort. The habit of the mind to look at our own faults through a magnifying glass is hard to overcome. While the *Yoga Vasistha* was written in India hundreds of years ago, it still points to an essential fact of life: we need to deal with our mind.

I thought of a friend who was struggling with her own thoughts that she was "not good enough," ready to throw in the towel and leave her job. It was so easy for her to list all the things that were not working. It was so hard to stop the negative thoughts and acknowledge her great virtues. Yet the moment she was reminded of her own strengths, she could pause, breathe, and pull herself out. Sometimes we need someone else to remind us, sometimes we remind ourselves, sometimes both.

While shaping this contemplation, I heard that someone had just published a children's book with the same storyline I was working on. I was filled with frustration. My thought was, "I didn't do enough to finish my own book." My initial reaction was self-negating. Then I reflected on the quote and my own goodness. Could I be courageous enough to say everything happens for the best? After a short time of disappointment, I forgave myself and simply said, "I'm doing the best I can."

Taking the contemplation deeper, I wondered if I could hold onto the awareness of my higher Self so thoroughly I might not even experience disappointment. A friend of mine always has ideas for new businesses. Whenever I let him know someone else is already doing a similar thing, he says, "Great. That means it's a good idea!" What a lovely way of holding onto one's own goodness, not succumbing to self-doubts.

Who are the real heroes? Are they the people whose only job right now is to fight a war no one likes? Could we stop the stream of violence against others and ourselves by taking a minute to breathe and remember our essentially good nature?

For the next week, become your own best friend. At any time, in any place, take a breath and remember your own goodness, your own divine nature. See what that does to the rest of your thoughts.

47

*True freedom comes about
through confidence in liberating any
and all thought states.*

Tsoknyi Rinpoche, *Fearless Simplicity*

In his book, the Tibetan teacher Tsoknyi Rinpoche teaches the practice of nonconceptual resting in the pure nature of the mind: emptiness and clarity. One of the most inspiring understandings he offers is a way to look at freedom and liberation.

In his Tibetan tradition, liberation means allowing thoughts or emotions to arise and subside on their own. Liberation happens moment by moment, thought by thought. Resting in one's own natural state of ease, not pushing things away, and not grasping them, thoughts can often self-liberate, or dissolve. Freedom comes from the recognition we don't have to be held captive by our thoughts or get caught up in them. Tsoknyi Rinpoche explains that we often walk around with a subtle fear of ourselves, a lack of trust in ourselves. Once we know we can free ourselves from the grip of thoughts, true freedom and confidence arise.

The practice of this is based on learning to see things as they are, rather than through the embellishments our ego adds. For example, someone was visiting my home this week. When I saw an unwashed pile of pots lying on the counter, my mind began creating judgments, irritation, and negativity towards my house guest. I turned my attention inward to the simple natural state of mind. From there, I could simply observe, "Oh, there are pots on the counter." All the extra commentary was totally unnecessary and dissolved. I was free in that moment and no further actions arose. This was perfect because later when I returned to the kitchen, all the pots had been washed. Imagine if I had started a scene, based on my knee-jerk response to my thoughts and emotions.

Tsoknyi Rinpoche writes, "Emotions have a right to arise, and you have the right not to cling to them. We should neither disturb the emotion's freedom nor our right not to be influenced and carried away. If we educate ourselves in this way, we become… flexible people who are unafraid of ourselves." We come to see that everything we presume to be true is simply a projection or dance of our minds.

Perhaps this is something you can try for yourself. Whenever strong emotions or distracting thoughts arise, simply rest in the state of openness and allow them to occur, with a sense of awareness. As you create some space between yourself and the thoughts as they arise, you may notice they self-liberate. Enjoy the freedom arising in that moment.

48

> *You could call contentment being in love with the moment, not just dutifully accepting it like an arranged marriage but passionately, rapturously embracing the eternal now as your soul mate.*
>
> Robert Johnson, *Contentment*

This week's focus for inquiry is based on a wonderful book by Robert Johnson, called *Contentment*. He describes two aspects of contentment: being just who we are, and finding contentment in our life just as it is.

Johnson writes, "Contentment can be found only in the middle place, the point where you are neither inflated nor deflated. It requires that you be who you are, no more and no less."

After reading those words, I began to observe the many ways in which I either let myself feel small or overemphasize being special. This can happen even during meditation. As I meditate, I can put myself down when I feel my meditation is shallow, or pat myself on the back when a wonderful state arises. What is meditation when I am neither no more nor no less than myself?

Johnson also writes, "Contentment grows out of the circumstances of life as you find it, in the very place where you currently exist." For me, that translates into not resisting whatever is in front of me, whether it is too much activity or too little. From lack of resistance, joy seems to arise by itself.

Recently, I was dealing with a small health challenge that temporarily reduced my energy for activity. At first, I was in a distressed state about it. Later, as I realized that the only way to heal was to rest, I began to revel in the freedom to just be still. I created a little mini-retreat for myself, listening to meditation tapes, writing in my journal, and sleeping. The feeling of contentment was quite surprising, as it arose despite being physically challenged.

For the next week, I invite you to investigate contentment by being who you are, living the life you have in this moment. It's a challenge I'm eager to take on. I hope you are, too.

49

Either give me enough wine or leave me alone
Now that I know how it is
to be with you in a constant conversation.

Rumi, "Now That I Know How It Is," *Open Secret*

Driving home from a retreat, I contemplated the subject of enlightenment. It may not be something you think about every day. It is hard for me to stay focused on it when I am busy paying bills, wondering where to live next or what to cook for dinner. However, a day or two of retreat is ideal for refocusing one's mind.

My contemplation was: What does the state of enlightenment look like? What would be different for me and others in my life? Here are some thoughts that arose.

Do I really "see" the people I interact with, especially the ones who are closest to me, the ones dearest to me? I reflected on a conversation I had with a friend, and thought how wonderful it would be to really see him as he is, not as I have created him. So often, after I know someone for a long time, he or she becomes frozen as an idea in my mind, and I interact with that idea. Enlightenment for me means seeing clearly from moment to moment, without the baggage of preconceived ideas or patterns of behavior.

Am I carrying the sense of responsibility for my life heavily or do I live life with ease, recognizing a divine power is orchestrating events? While thinking about moving, I found myself getting uptight. Yet every change I have ever made has been filled with grace. In an enlightened state, I would be in constant conversation with that unseen power, making decisions and taking action with lightness and ease.

Do I really experience my true nature as free, as already liberated, or do I believe in the small manifestation I call Laura? Some days, I get caught up in my own dramas. Other times, I can look upon my life as a great play. In an enlightened state, I would play the role of Laura, simultaneously knowing it is not real.

As Rumi points out, we already know what it's like to be "in constant conversation." However, I find it helpful to name the behaviors to which I aspire, as they inspire me to further practice. Are they just concepts? Perhaps. But, for me, some concepts can be a helpful way of moving forward. Then, like the boat that carries one across a river, they can be put down on the other side.

I offer you this contemplation: What does enlightenment, or self-realization, mean to you? What would it look like to be in constant conversation with the Divine? What practices are you doing to take you closer to who you really are?

50

One's own thought is one's world.
What a person thinks is what he becomes.
That is the eternal mystery.

The Maitri Upanishad

On Sunday, the final game for the World Cup of Soccer ended in overtime. One single penalty goal separated the winning team from the second-place team, after a grueling 100+ minutes of great soccer. One team experienced ecstasy, the other the agony of defeat. You could see it on their faces. But it could just as easily have been the other way around. In the end, although you could say it was a goal that made the difference, it was also a thought: "I am a winner" or "I am a loser." When the negative thought prevails, all the positives go out the window. What about all the victorious games that led the second-place team to the finals? What about the amazing way they played in the final game? It was all gone in a split second.

The power of one thought is so amazing. We don't have to lose the World Cup to recognize how we undermine our own goodness. For example, we might be living a life of genuine service and yet be plagued with self-doubt: "Why aren't I competing for high-pressure jobs to earn lots of money?" One thought can make the difference between undermining ourselves and knowing, as the fourteenth century Sufi mystic and poet Hafiz says, "everything you do is sacred."

※

For the next week, I invite you to recognize the power of thought in affirming your daily life. Take any scenario you are currently living. If you find yourself engaging in self-doubt, see if you can you find a positive thought that is self-affirming and choose it over any one of a million self-negating thoughts. If our world is made of our thoughts, why not choose to think well?

51

Learn what dwells in man, what is not given unto man, and what men live by.

Leo Tolstoy, *Walk in the Light*

In a short story by Leo Tolstoy, an angel is sent to earth and told he can return to heaven when he learns the three things stated above. As I contemplated them, I also considered the difference between knowing the answer versus experiencing the answer. I might agree with Tolstoy's answers, but does it come from my experience of life?

What dwells in a person? Another way to say that is, what shines through people in the most critical of situations? What can we see when we look below the surface of a person? Tolstoy says, love. Is it possible to see love in every person we meet?

What is not given to a person? Perhaps there is a better translation from Russian. I might word it, what can a person never know? Tolstoy says, "It is not given to man to know his own needs." He gives an example of someone who orders new shoes, but dies suddenly. We don't know when death will come, so we don't really know what we need from one day to the next. This is a great contemplation and practice. What is it like to live open to not-knowing?

What do people live by? In this question, I find the greatest alignment with my own experience. Tolstoy says we live by love. For me, even a spiritual practice such as meditation is fueled by love. Without love, meditation is dry, life is dry. What is your experience?

Tolstoy concludes his story with this: "He who has love, is in God, and God is in him, for God is love." We have so many definitions for God. Could it be as simple as that?

For the next week, I invite you to contemplate each of these questions, and perhaps compare what you find with Tolstoy's conclusions. Enjoy the contemplation.

52

*You are — we all are — the beloved
of the Beloved, and in every moment, in
every event of your life, the Beloved is
whispering to you exactly what you
need to hear and know.*

Rumi, *Light Upon Light*

Last week, on my birthday, a friend sent me a book of Rumi's writings. As I read it, here's what I wrote in my journal: "Imagine I'm a lamp unplugged... and you gently take the plug and put it back into the socket, where it used to be. And voilà, I burn brightly again. Everything in me is singing with energy and light, drenched with love. I turn page after page in the Rumi book, and find God and Love waiting. And I think, where have I been? Days spent in endless spiritual practices and quests, and none of them come close to this: being plugged back into my heart, into God, into the mystery of the search, into love."

What happened? That's the mystery. However, I can say that through the past weeks, as I have been making efforts to be responsible about my life, the fact I am the "beloved of the Beloved" got lost somewhere along the way. I have been keeping company with my mind, rather than my heart. My ego was making all the effort. Reading Rumi, all the striving ceased. I am not alone, and have never been. Everything I need is waiting for me.

What does this look like in daily life? As an example, I was feeling undervalued by a recent job offer. I felt I wasn't appreciated for who I was, based on the amount of money offered. In fact, no amount of money can buy what I really am — the beloved of the Beloved. As one of my mentors pointed out, if I truly know my pricelessness, then I am free. I can choose to take less money because that is what is offered, even while knowing I am worth far more. Or I can turn it down without hard feelings, because my sense of worth has not been touched. It is so ingrained in us to base our value on what others say it is. When I sit in Rumi's company, nothing in the material world can ever diminish my value. I am the beloved of the Beloved. I am free.

I offer you Rumi's words as a contemplation for the week. Can you reconnect with the mystery of your relationship with the Divine, and in doing so, let go? Rumi says, "In this world and in all others, everything happens by His Will, and for purposes hidden in Mystery. Love, and Love only, will lead you to the placeless place where you know this simply, and so smile inwardly and fear no more."

Closing Blessings

From the Buddhist Metta (Loving-Kindness) prayer

May you know happiness
and the source of happiness
May you know peace,
as everyone wishes to know peace
May you be free from suffering,
and be strong and healthy
May you be safe and protected
from inner and outer harm.

From the Indian Universal Prayer

May everyone surmount their difficulties.
May everyone see only auspicious sights.
May everyone, everywhere be glad.
Peace, Peace, Peace.

Bibliography & References

Amiel, Henri Frédéric. *Amiel's Journal: The Journal Intime of Henri-Frédéric Amiel.* BiblioBazaar, 2006.

Aurelius, Marcus. *Meditations.* London, England: Penquin Books, Ltd, 2006.

Balsekar, Ramesh. *Duet of One: The Ashtavakra Gita Dialogue.* Redondo Beach, California: Advaita Press, 1989

Barks, Coleman, John Moyne. *Open Secret: Versions of Rumi.* Boston, Massachusetts: Shambhala Publications, 1989.

Barks, Coleman, John Moyne. *The Essential Rumi.* San Francisco, California: HarperCollins 1996.

Berry, Wendell. *Collected Poems.* North Point Press, 1987.

Berry, Wendell. *Hannah Coulter.* Shoemaker & Hoard, 2004.

Bodhidhamma, Bhante *Buddhadharma Magazine*, Spring, 2007

Chidvilasananda, Gurumayi. *Sadhana of the Heart, Volume I.* South Fallsburg, New York: SYDA Foundation, 2006.

Chidvilasananda, Gurumayi. "Through the Eye of the Heart." *Smile, Smile, Smile! Poems by.* South Fallsburg, New York: SYDA Foundation, 1999. Page 39. Reprinted with permission.

Chodron, Pema. *When Things Fall Apart: Heart Advice for Difficult Times.* Boston, Massachusetts: Shambhala Publications, 1997.

Collins, Billy. "On Turning Ten." *Sailing Alone Around the Room.* New York: Random House, Inc, 2001.

Dickinson, Emily. *The Complete Poems of Emily Dickinson.* Boston, Massachusetts: Little, Brown, and Company, 1960.

Dostoyevsky, Fyodor. *The Brothers Karamazov.* New York: Ferrar, Straus and Giroux, 1990.

Griffin, Howard John. *Follow the Ecstasy, the Hermitage Years of Thomas Merton.* Maryknoll, New York: Orbis Books, 1993.

Harvey, Andrew. *Light Upon Light: Inspirations from Rumi.* New York: Jeremy P. Tarcher/Penguin, 2004.

Hass, Robert, editor. *The Essential Haiku:Versions of Basho, Buson and Issa.* New York: Harper Collins, 1994.

Jampolsky, Gerald. *Love is Letting Go of Fear.* Berkeley, California: Celestial Arts, 1979.

Johnson, Robert, Jerry Ruhl. *Contentment A Way to True Happiness.* New York: Harper Collins, 2000.

Johnson, Robert. *Owning Your Own Shadow.* New York: Harper Collins, 1993.

Kabat-Zinn, Jon. *Full Catastrophe Living: Using the Wisdom of Your Body and Mind to Face Stress, Pain and Illness.* New York: Dell, 1990.

Kingsley, Peter and Maria. As Far As Longing Can Reach. (2006). *Parabola, Volume 31 (no. 2 Summer 2006)* p59.

Kongtrul, Dzigar. *It's Up to You: The Practice of Self-Reflection on the Buddhist Path.* Boston, Massachusetts: Shambhala Publications, 2005.

Kubler-Ross, Elisabeth. *On Life After Death.* Berkeley, California: Celestial Arts, 2008.

Ladinsky, Daniel. *I Heard God Laughing: Renderings of Hafiz.* Walnut Creek, CA: Sufism Reoriented, 1996.

Lao Tzu. *Tao Te Ching: A New English Version* translated by Stephen Mitchell. New York: Harper Perennial Classics, 2006.

May, Gerald. *The Awakened Heart: Opening Yourself to the Love You Need.* New York: Harper Collins, 1993.

Monks of New Skete. *In the Spirit of Happiness: A Books of Spiritual Wisdom.* Back Bay Books, 2001.

Muktananda, Swami. *From the Finite to the Infinite.* South Fallsburg, New York: SYDA Foundation, 1994. page 422. Reprinted with permission.

Muktananda, Swami. *Play of Consciousness: A Spiritual Autobiography.* South Fallsburg, New York: SYDA Foundation, 1994.

Nisargadatta, Mauric Frydman, translator. *I Am That: Talks with Sri Nisargadatta Maharaj.* India: Chetana Private, Ltd, 1999.

Prabhavananda, Swami, Christopher Isherwood. *Bhagavad Gita: The Song of God.* London, England: New American Library, 2002.

Prabhavananda, Swami, Frederick Manchester, translator. *The Upanishads: Breath of the Eternal.* New York: Signet, 1957.

Plato, Hugh Tedennick (trans). *The Last Days of Socrates.* London, England: Penguin, 1954.

Porter, Bill (translator). *The Heart Sutra (Prajnaparamita).* Shoemaker and Hoard, 2004.

Seng-Ts'an. *Hsin-Hsin Ming.* White Pine Press, 2001.

Tagore, Rabindranath. *Songs of Kabir.* York Beach, Maine: Samuel Weiser, Inc., 1995.

Tolstoy, Leo. *Walk in the Light and Twenty-three Tales.* Maryknoll, New York: Orbis Books, 2003.

Trungpa, Chogyam. *Shambhala: The Sacred Path of the Warrior.* Boston, Massachusetts: Shambhala Publications, 1984.

Trungpa, Chogyam. *Training the Mind and Cultivating Loving-Kindness.* Boston, Massachusetts: Shambhala Publications, 1993.

Tsoknyi Rinpoche. *Fearless Simplicity: The Dzogchen Way of Living Freely in a Complex World.* North Atlantic Books, 2003

Venkateshananda, Swami. *The Supreme Yoga: A Translation of the Yoga Vasishta.* India: Motilal Banarsidass, 2003.

Index of Quotations

Both the beneficial and the pleasurable present themselves to man. The wise, having examined both, prefer the beneficial to the pleasurable. *Katha Upanishad* p36

Come, join the courageous, Who have no choice But to bet their entire world That indeed, Indeed, God is Real. Hafiz p92

Drive all blames into one. Atisha p58

Either give me enough wine or leave me alone, now that I know how it is to be with you in a constant conversation. Rumi p112

Enlightenment is not imagining figures of light but making the darkness conscious. Carl Jung p102

Every day is a good day. Um-mon Zenji p16

Fear always distorts our perceptions and confuses us as to what is going on. Love is the total absence of fear. Gerald Jampolsky p24

Forgiveness is the key to action and freedom. Hannah Arendt p64

He whom one loves will always be near. If you have entrusted body and soul, there can be no parting. Kabir p68

I always live in this state: I am not this body; I am Consciousness. I lose myself in this awareness most of the time. Sometimes I may come out of this awareness but I know how to get back into it. Swami Muktananda p53

I know the way you can get/ If you have not had a drink from Love's Hands. Hafiz p56

If we make our goal to live a life of compassion and unconditional love, then the world will indeed become a garden where all kinds of flowers can bloom and grow. Elisabeth Kubler-Ross p86

Instead of trying to see everything through the prism of the mind, let the brilliant rays of the eye of the heart reflect everything in its true colors. Gurumayi Chidvilasananda p96

It seems only yesterday I used to believe/ there was nothing beneath my skin but light./ If you cut me I would shine./ But now when I fall upon the sidewalks of life,/ I scrape my knees. I bleed. Billy Collins p30

Just remember you can endure anything your mind can make endurable, by treating it as in your interest to do so. Marcus Aurelius p32

Kindle the light in your own hearts, and in turn the flame will pass on and light the hearts of others as well. Turn the light of love on those who are in darkness, and touch them with a joyful smile. Buddha p74

Learn what dwells in man, what is not given unto man, and what men live by. Leo Tolsoy p116

Let yourself be silently drawn by the stronger pull of what you really love. Rumi p38

Love does not seek her own way, is not easily provoked, is not anxious to suspect evil... bears all things, believes all things, hopes all things, endures all things. St. Paul p104

Love the animals, love the plants, love everything. If you love everything, you will perceive the divine mystery in things. Once you perceive it, you will begin to comprehend it better everyday. And you will come to love the whole world with an all-embracing love. Fyodor Dostoyevsky p94

Mornings I hear the sounds of the world; evenings I hear the sounds of the world. Robert Aitken p54

Nothing is so strong as gentleness, nothing so gentle as real strength. St. Francis de Sales p34

One is not a hero who defeats a mighty army. The true hero is the one who crosses the ocean know as the mind and the senses. You are your own friend, you are your own enemy. Yoga Vasishta p106

One's own thought is one's world. What a person thinks is what he becomes. That is the eternal mystery. The Maitri Upanishad p114

Our longing, if we dare to follow it all the way, is what turns us inside out until we find the sun and the moon and stars inside. Peter and Maria Kingsley p90

Sometimes too I could see that love is a great room with lots of doors, where we are invited to knock and come in. Though it contains all the world, the sun, moon and stars, it is so small as to be also in our hearts. It is in the hearts of those who choose to come in. Wendell Berry p44

Take a music bath once or twice a week for a few seasons, and you will find that it is to the soul what the water-bath is to the body. Oliver Wendell Holmes p18

The capacity for paradox is the measure of spiritual strength and the surest sign of maturity. To advance from opposition (always a quarrel) to paradox (always holy) is to make a leap of consciousness. Robert Johnson p88

The man who has no inner life is the slave of his surroundings, as the barometer is the obedient servant of the air at rest, and the weathercock is the humble servant of the air in motion. Henri Frédéric Amiel p46

The meditation orientation is not about fixing pain or making it better. It's about looking deeply, into the nature of pain—making use of it in certain ways that might allow us to grow. Jon Kabat-Zinn p48

The soul should always stand ajar, ready to welcome the ecstatic experience. Emily Dickinson p66

The Way is easy for those who harbor no preferences. Seng Ts'an p22

The world of dew is the world of dew, and yet, and yet – Issa p84

There is nothing more beautiful and freeing than living with conscious dedication to love. Gerald May p62

Through the practice of meditation, we begin to find that within ourselves there is no fundamental complaint about anything or anyone at all. Chogyam Trungpa p82

To follow the spiritual path authentically is to die to our old rigidities, turning long-cherished opinions and ingrained attitudes upside down… to see beyond delusion to reality… challenging the way we look at everything. Monks of New Skete p78

To go in the dark with a light is to know the light. To know the dark, go dark. Go without sight… and know that the dark, too, blooms and sings, and is traveled by dark feet and dark wings. Wendell Berry p100

Tranquility means the absence of resistance to the experience of the present moment. Ramesh Balsekar p60

True freedom comes about through confidence in liberating any and all thought states. Tsoknyi Rinpoche p108

We are visitors on this planet. We are here for ninety or one hundred years at the very most. During that period, we must try to do something good, something useful with our lives. If you contribute to other people's happiness, you will find the true goal, the true meaning of life. H.H. the 14th Dalai Lama p20

We cannot stay home all our lives – we must present ourselves to the world, and look upon it as an adventure. Beatrix Potter p98

We must always change, renew, rejuvenate ourselves; otherwise we harden. Goethe p50

What we consider to be our personality is only a collection of habits that are driving us to our destiny. Bhante Bodhidamma p76

When effort is needed, effort will appear. When effortless becomes essential, it will assert itself. You need not push life about. Nisargadatta p70

When one gets older, one realizes the futility of a life wasted in argument when it should be given entirely to love. Thomas Merton p80

When you are content to be simply yourself, and don't compare or compete, everybody will respect you. Lao Tzu p40

Without ego as our primary reference point, mind is naturally open, unconfused, and able to enjoy everything without judgment. Dzigar Kongtrul p42

Without going out of your door, you can know the ways of the world. Without peeping through your window, you can see the Ways of Heaven. Lao Tzu p26

You are — we all are — the beloved of the Beloved, and in every moment, in every event of your life, the Beloved is whispering to you exactly what you need to hear and know. Rumi p118

You could call contentment being in love with the moment, not just dutifully accepting it like an arranged marriage but passionately, rapturously embracing the eternal now as your soul mate. Robert Johnson p110

You have to pay salutations to your own obstacles, hindrances, because otherwise there would be no notion of freedom and enlightenment. Dzigar Kongtrul p28

You think to make your living from tailoring...Rumi p72

www.ingramcontent.com/pod-product-compliance
Lightning Source LLC
Chambersburg PA
CBHW072336300426
44109CB00042B/1648